Gardens & Gardening on 1

CW00880815

A practical handbook and reference guide to horticulture online

Internet Handbooks

Many other titles in preparation

Gardens & Gardening

on the internet

A practical handbook and reference guide
to horticulture online

Judith & Graham Lawlor

www.internet-handbooks.co.uk

First published in 2000 by Internet Handbooks, a Division of International Briefings Ltd, Plymbridge House, Estover Road, Plymouth PL6 7PY, United Kingdom.

Customer services tel: (01752) 202301
Orders fax: (01752) 202333
Customer services email: cservs@plymbridge.com
Distributors web site: http://www.plymbridge.com
Internet Handbooks web site: http://www.internet-handbooks.co.uk

Note: The contents of this book are offered for the purposes of general guidance only and no liability can be accepted for any loss or expense incurred as a result of relying in particular circumstances on statements made in this book. Readers are advised to check the current position with the appropriate authorities before entering into personal arrangements.

Case studies in this book are entirely fictional and any resemblance to real persons or organisations is entirely coincidental.

Printed and bound by The Cromwell Press Ltd, Trowbridge, Wiltshire.

Contents

Contents

List of illustrations

Preface

Gardening is one of the most relaxing and satisfying of past-times. It is delightful to be able to place seeds into the ground and grow plants from them, and it is an excellent way of staying active and productive.

We work as a team, Judith as the horticultural expert, and Graham contributing his professional experience of the internet. We have sought to combine our interests in the production of this book.

Gardening means working with nature. The Earth is a living organism which we should nourish and care for, both for our own sakes and for those who come after us. The book covers gardening organically; if you have never tried this, why not give it a go?

A number of commercial firms are mentioned in these pages. We have not sought or received any financial or other benefit from them. They have been selected in the belief that their products and services may be of interest. If you have any comments about the products or service you receive from any of them, favourable or otherwise, we would be very glad to hear from you.

The internet is a vast inter-connection of computers that spans the globe. It is a massive development that places vast quantities of information at your fingertips. Don't worry if you have never surfed the internet before. By the time you have finished this book, you will think nothing of using the new medium. If you are new to the internet, please refer to the Appendix at the back of the book. There is some basic help to get you started.

We are convinced that, during the next decade, the internet will revolutionise the way we live and work. It will enable us to do far more than ever before. As gardeners, it will give us far more control over the nature and style of the products that we buy, and it offers an amazing gateway to getting help and information from anywhere in the world.

The internet means you can join a community of thousands even millions – of fellow enthusiasts online. It offers a chance to develop new friendships, based on shared interests, with other gardeners anywhere in the world. Make the most of it, and happy surfing!

Judith and Graham Lawlor

lawlor@internet-handbooks.co.uk

1 Searching for information

In this chapter we will explore:

▶ *searching the internet*
▶ *tips for searching*
▶ *bookmarking your favourite web sites*
▶ *search engines and directories*
▶ *search utilities*
▶ *portal sites for gardening and horticulture*

. . . .

Searching the internet

The usual way to look up something on the internet is to go to the web site of a well-known search engine or internet directory. These services are free and open to everyone.

▶ *Search engines* – These are also known as spiders or crawlers. They have highly sophisticated search tools that automatically seek out sites across the internet. These trawl through and index literally millions of pages of internet content. As a result they often find information that is not listed in directories.

▶ *Internet directories* – These are developed and compiled by people. Authors submit their site details and they are assigned to certain areas on the directory.

The browser that your ISP provides should have certain search engines on it, ready for you to use, but you can go to and use any of the search engines listed below, and use them yourself.

Most people refer to directories as search engines and lump the two together. For the purposes of this book, we will refer to them all as search engines. Popular search engines have now become big web sites in their own right, usually combining many useful features. As well as search boxes where you can type key words to summarise what you are looking for, you will usually also find handy directories of information, news, email and many other services. There are hundreds if not thousands of search engines freely available. The biggest and best known are AltaVista, Excite, Infoseek, Lycos and Yahoo! (the most popular of all).

Tips for searching

1. If you want general information, try Yahoo! or AltaVista first. For specific information, try one of the major search engines.
2. If you do a search for UK plants, the search engine will search for UK, and search for plants quite separately. This may produce details of the UK Olympic team, for example not what you want. The way to avoid this is to enclose your key words in quotation marks. If you type in

'UK plants' then only web sites with that combination of words will be listed for you.

3. George Boole was a 19th-century English mathematician who worked on logic. He gave his name to Boolean operators – simple words like AND, OR and NOT. If you include these words in your searches, it should narrow down the results, for example: 'Plants AND UK NOT USA'. However, don't go overboard and restrict the search too much, or you may get few or no results.

4. Try out several different search engines, and see which one you like the best. Or you could obtain the handy little search utility called Web Ferret (see below): if the information is not on one search engine, Web Ferret can usually find it on one or more of the others.

Bookmarking your favourite web sites

Your browser (usually Internet Explorer or Netscape Navigator) enables you to save the addresses of any web sites you specially like, and may want to revisit. These are called 'bookmarks' in Netscape, or 'favorites' in Internet Explorer (US spelling). In either case, simply click on the relevant button on your browser's toolbar, Bookmarks or Favorites as the case may be. This produces a little drop-down menu that you click on to add the site concerned. When you want to revisit that site later, click again on the same button; then click the name of the web site you bookmarked, and within a few seconds it will open for you.

Fig. 1. To save a web page you might want to revisit, you can bookmark it. In Internet Explorer (top), click Favorites then Add to Favorites. In Netscape (bottom), click Bookmarks then Add to Bookmarks.

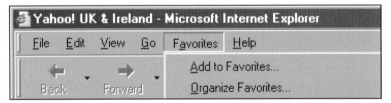

Search engines

AltaVista

http://www.altavista.com

http://www.altavista.co.uk

AltaVista is one of the most popular search sites among web users world wide. It contains details of millions of web pages on its massive and ever-growing database. You can either follow the trails of links from its home page, or (better) type in your own key words into its search box. You can even search in about 25 different languages. On the UK home page, click on Recreation and Travel, then Gardens & Gardening.

Fig. 2. AltaVista is one of the most popular search sites on the internet. With its search facility, and directory listings, it is easy to use, though equally easy to become over-whelmed with irrelevant links.

Ask Jeeves
http://www.ask.com

Ask Jeeves offers a slightly different approach to searches. It invites you to ask questions on the internet just as you would of a friend or colleague. For example you could type in something like: 'Where can I find out about orchids?' Jeeves retrieves the information, drawing from a knowledge base of millions of standard answers.

Fig. 3. The Ask Jeeves search engine takes a slightly different approach. It invites you to ask it questions (by typing), just as you would ask questions of a friend or colleague.

Electronic Yellow Pages
http://www.eyp.co.uk

These electronic yellow pages are organised on the same lines as the paper edition. Just type in the details of the information you need – anything from garden centres to horticulture – and it quickly searches for appropriate services in your local area.

Excite
http://www.excite.com
http://www.excite.co.uk

Excite is another of the top ten search engines and directories on the internet. To refine your search, simply click the check boxes next to the words you want to add and then click the Search Again button. There are separate Excite home pages for several different countries and cultures including Australia, Chinese, France, German, Italy, Japan, Netherlands,

Searching for information. . . . .

Spain, Sweden, and the USA. On the UK home page try typing in Gardening into the search box.

Global On-line Directory
http://www.god.co.uk
Launched in 1996, GOD is fairly unusual among search engines in that it is UK-based, and aims to be a premier European search service. Features of the site include a 'global search' where you can search for web sites by country, state, province, county or even city by city, narrowing down the information for a more focused result.

Google
http://www.google.com
A new and innovative search site is Google. It matches your query to the text in its index, to find relevant pages. For instance, when analysing a page for indexing, it looks at what the pages linking to that page have to say about it, so the rating partly depends on what others say about it.

HotBot
http://hotbot.lycos.com
This is an impressive, very popular, and well-classified search engine and directory, now associated with Lycos (see below). On the home page, click Travel & Recreation, then Gardens, for well over 3,000 gardening links.

Infoseek (Go Network)
http://infoseek.go.com
In 1994, the American 'netpreneur' Steve Kirsch founded Infoseek with the mission of helping people unleash the power of the internet. Infoseek pioneered a suite of powerful, high-quality and easy-to-use search tools. Infoseek is one of the leading search engines on the internet.

Internet Address Finder
http://www.iaf.net
The IAF is used by millions of web users for searching and finding the

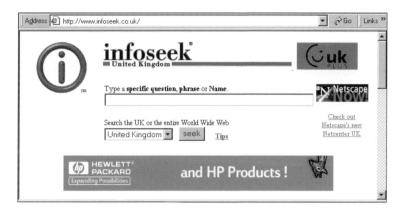

Fig. 5. The very popular Infoseek search engine is among the top six on the internet.

names, email addresses, and now Intel Internet video phone contacts, of other users world wide. With millions of addresses it is one of the most comprehensive email directories on the internet. By registering, you will also enable others to find you.

Internet Public Library
http://www.ipl.org/ref
The 'Ask-a-Question' service at the Internet Public Library is experimental. The librarians who work here are mostly volunteers with other full-time librarian jobs. Your question is received at the IPL Reference Centre and the mail is reviewed once a day and questions are forwarded to a place where all the librarians can see them and answer them. Replies are sent as soon as possible, advising whether your question has been accepted or rejected. If it has been accepted, you should receive an answer to your question in two to seven days.

List of Search Engines
http://www.search-engine-index.co.uk
This enterprising British site offers a free list of hundreds of search engines, covering different topics. There are search engines for software, multiple searches, email and news, law, TV, film, music, the press, images and technology manufacturers, as well as web, commercial, localised and word reference science search engines.

Looksmart
http://www.looksmart.com
This is another good directory with something in the region of 350 000 catalogued sites. You can find it on the Netscape Net Search Page. If your search is not successful, you are redirected to AltaVista.

Lycos
http://www.lycos.com
http://www.lycos.co.uk
Lycos is another of the top ten worldwide web search engines. Lycos is the name for a type of ground spider. It searches document titles, headings, links, and keywords, and returns the first few words of each page it

Searching for information...

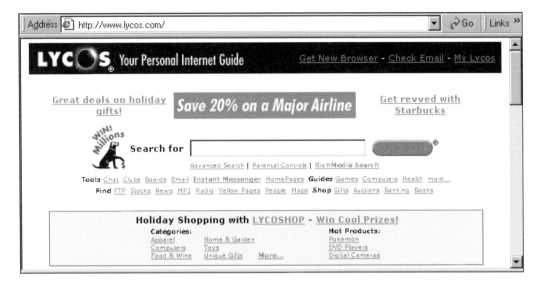

Fig. 6. Lycos was one of the earliest search and navigation sites on the internet. It is used by millions of people every day.

indexes for your search. Founded in 1995, Lycos was one of the earliest search and navigation sites designed to help people find information more easily and quickly on the world wide web. The core technology was developed at Carnegie Mellon University. In 1997, with Bertelsmann, it has launched Lycos sites in 11 European countries.

Metacrawler
http://www.metacrawler.com
MetaCrawler was originally developed by Erik Selberg and Oren Etzioni at the University of Washington, and released to the internet in 1995. In response to each user query, it incorporates results from all the top search engines. It collates results, eliminates duplication, scores the results and provides the user with a list of relevant sites.

SavvySearch
http://www.savvysearch.com
Owned by CNET, SavvySearch is one of the leading providers of meta-search services. Its search engine offers a single point of access to hundreds of different search engines, guides, archives, libraries, and other resources. You type in a keyword query which is then immediately sent out to all appropriate internet search engines. The results are gathered and displayed within a few seconds.

Scoot Yahoo!
http://scoot.yahoo.co.uk
Yahoo! has combined with the British directory Scoot to offer an excellent search facility for those looking for UK-oriented information, businesses and organisations. Once you have found the organisation you are looking for you can click straight into their web site if they have one. There is a link on the home page to Home & Garden.

Search.com
http://search.cnet.com
This service is run by CNET, one of the world's leading new-media companies. From the home page you can click an A-Z list option which displays an archive of all its search engines. The list is long, but just about everything you need to master the web is there. You can search yellow pages, phone numbers, email addresses, message boards, software downloads, and easily do all kinds of special searches.

Starting Point MetaSearch
http://www.stpt.com/search.html
This is a powerful metasearcher that puts numerous high-quality, popular, and comprehensive search tools – general and category specific – at your fingertips.

UK Directory
http://www.ukdirectory.co.uk
This is a useful directory listing to UK-based web sites. You can browse it or search it. It has a well-classified subject listing. UK Directory is simple and intuitive to use. You don't need to know the name of the company, service or person to find the things you are interested in. Just look in the category that best suits your needs. It is as easy to use as a telephone directory.

UK Index
http://www.ukindex.co.uk
This is another directory of sites in or about the UK. It assigns sites to broad categories to help you with searching. The depth of information seems variable.

UK Plus
http://www.ukplus.co.uk
The parent company of this UK-oriented search engine and database is Daily Mail & General Trust – owners of the *Daily Mail,* the *Mail on Sunday, London Evening Standard* and a number of UK regional newspapers – so it draws on a rich tradition of quality publishing. It has built a vast store of web site reviews written by a team of experienced journalists. Although it concentrates on UK web sites, you will also find many from all over the world which are included because it feels they are likely to be of interest to British readers.

UK Yellow Web Directory
http://www.yell.co.uk
This site is operated by the yellow pages division of British Telecom. It is indexed 'by humans' and is searchable. A number of non-UK sites are included in the database. There is also an A to Z company listing, but note that companies whose names begin with 'The' are listed under T. A Business Compass lists 'the best' business internet resources, with links and brief descriptions.

Searching for information...

Fig. 7. Yell is a free online service for looking up business web sites and addresses. It is run by the yellow pages division of British Telecom.

Webcrawler
http://webcrawler.com
Webcrawler is a fast worker and returns an impressive list of links. It analyses the full text of documents, allowing the searcher to locate key words which may have been buried deep within a document's text. Webcrawler is now part of Excite. On the home page, click Home & Real Estate, then Garden & Landscape.

World Email Directory
http://www.worldemail.com
This site is dedicated to email, email, more email, finding people and locating businesses and organisations. WED has access to an estimated 18 million email addresses and more than 140 million business and phone addresses worldwide. Here you'll find everything from email software, to email list servers, many worldwide email databases, business, telephone and fax directories and a powerful email search engine.

Yahoo!
http://www.yahoo.com
http://www.yahoo.co.uk
Yahoo! was the first substantial internet directory, and continues to be one of the best for free general searching. It contains millions of links categorised by subject. You can 'drill down' through the categories to

Fig. 8. Very functional and plain in appearance, Yahoo! is still the largest and most popular internet directory and search engine on the web.

find what you want, or carry out your own searches using keywords. The site also offers world news, sport, weather, email, chat, retailing facilities, clubs and many other features. Yahoo! is probably one of the search engines and directories you will use time after time, as do millions of people every day.

Search utilities

Bonzi Buddy
http://www.bonzi.com
Bonzi Buddy is not a search engine or directory as such, but a useful search facility. A little parrot 'flies' around your desktop. It is a free download and can be quite fun. It can ' learn' which type of sites you like to use and search out new sites for you. 'Peedi' even talks and tells jokes (very badly). You have been warned!

WebFerret
http://www.ferretsoft.com
WebFerret is an excellent functional search utility. You can key in your query offline, and when you connect it searches the web until it has collected all the references you have specified – up to 9,999 if you wish. WebFerret can query ten or more search engines simultaneously and discards duplicate results. The search engines it queries include AltaVista, Yahoo, Infoseek, Excite, and others. You can immediately visit the URLs it finds, even while WebFerret is still running. The program is free, and simplicity itself. It only takes a few minutes to download from FerretSoft. Highly recommended.

Fig. 9. Produced by FerretSoft, Web Ferret is an excellent and very easy-to-use search utility program. It take the hard work out of searching by using nine or more top search engines simultaneously.

Portal sites for gardening and horticulture

▶ *About portal sites* – Portal means gateway. It is a web site designed to be a starting point for your web experience each time you go online. Portals often serve as general information points and offer news, weather and other information that you can customise to your own needs. Yahoo! (see above) is a good example of a general portal site. As the internet has expanded, there are now all kinds of useful portal sites for specialist areas, for example gardening and horticulture. Visiting any of these sites will give you quick access to hundreds

– and sometimes thousands of links, organised in a generally user-friendly way.

Australian Gardens
http://www.crosswinds.net/ ~ ausgardens
This is the official 'home' for members of the Australian Gardens mailing list. 'We offer help, a look at our own gardens, tips, and how-to-join information.'

e-Garden (UK)
http://www.e-garden.co.uk
Launched in September 1999, this is an impressive source of advice, news, a garden events calendar, competitions and online garden shop-

Fig. 10. e-Garden. Portal site sites like these are a very handy way of exploring any subject on the internet, such as gardening.

ping, with quality gardening journalism, images, gardening databases and e-publications. It provides a home shopping facility for plants, seeds, bulbs and other products from leading suppliers. The site includes a Latin plant-name translator which can change some 72,000 names from Latin to English and back again. e-Garden is the brainchild of Brian Vass, former Head of Information Technology at the Royal Horticultural Society where he was responsible for developing the RHS web site.

Garden Book
http://www.gardenbook.com
With over 2,000 gardening titles, Garden Book claims to be the largest and most specialised bookstore for gardeners on the internet. If we don't have it, ask. 'If it is anywhere, we'll find it'.

Garden Centre
http://www.gardencentre.co.uk
This attractively designed web site offers seasonal tips, a diary of garden events, and links to fencing and solar fountain suppliers. It also offers 'telegardening' which it describes as the 'ultimate leisure inactivity for the committed mouse potato'. You can view, tend or water the telegarden

using a robot arm with an attached video camera, all from the comfort of your favourite chair

Garden Links
http://www.gardenlinks.ndo.co.uk
This is a substantial directory for UK gardening suppliers, gardens to visit, advice, gardening books, wildlife gardens, garden plants and more.

Garden Planet
http://www.worldleader.com/garden/index.htm
This is a site of 'web resources for friendly gardeners'. There's an index to bookmark if you are looking for garden and gardening resources, flowers, vegetables, and herbs.

The Gardeners Network
http://www.gardenersnet.com/index.htm
Garden Web hosts discussion forums, garden exchanges, articles, contests, a plant database, a huge garden-related glossary and online catalogues. It is home to the Calendar of Garden Events, The Rosarian, Wild Flowers and sister sites in Europe and Australia. It aims to combine interactivity with imaginative content and a user-friendly interface. Here, 'you will find a listing of the many gardening resources available at Garden Web. If you would like to be added to our mailing list so you can hear about future updates to our gardening sites, simply fill in your email address below and click on the subscribe button.' Garden Web serves more than 3 million page views a month.

Garden World
http://www.gardenworld.co.uk
This useful site covers UK garden centres, gardening topics, events, competitions, recruitment, and gardening links. With a listing of over 1,000 UK garden centres, you can explore which centres are closest to you and what services, facilities, plants and garden products are offered by each garden centre. The site features various new garden products and suppliers.

Fig. 11. The web site of Garden World, another very useful portal site for gardeners, especially in the UK.

Gardening 365
http://www.oxalis.co.uk
This is a useful general portal site to British gardening. You can find out about plants, and gardening events in the UK, search the web, place a classified ad, or discuss gardening topics. The site includes clickable maps with dots representing gardens open to the public; click on any of these – there are hundreds to reveal more detailed information.

Gardening Launch Pad
http://www.tpoint.net/neighbor
This is a very enterprising and well-organised list of gardening sites all over the world. It offers more than 4,000 (mostly non-commercial) links to every imaginable aspect of gardening and horticulture. You're sure to find the answer somewhere here.

Fig. 12. Gardening Launch Pad: this is another excellent gardening portal which provides more than 4,000 well-organised gardening links.

Gardening New Zealand
http://www.links.co.nz/family/garden.htm
This is a site with lots of great gardening links, both for New Zealand and around the world.

Gardening UK
http://www.gardening-uk.com
This is a UK-only site for nurseries to advertise their wares. There are cat-alogues for nurseries and specialist growers, greenhouses, garden accessories, furniture, and fencing, seed merchants and seed specialists, landscaping, consultancy, courses, and tree surgeons.

Gardening Sites Directory
http://www.gardening-sites.swinternet.co.uk
This is a rather basic-looking directory of gardeners' and commercial gar-dening web sites. There are some useful and relevant links, but you may have to hunt around a little to find what you want.

Expert Gardener
http://www.expertgardener.com
This site started life as iGarden but has gone on to bigger and better things. Alan Titchmarsh and Charlie Dimmock are both involved in this

site, which offers lots of interest. We have not met the two personalities but they have done a great deal in keeping gardening popular and on the screen, and they both know what they are talking about. The site itself is a delight. We particularly liked the fact that you can register where you live and so receive up to date weather forecasts. This is an ideal support service for the dedicated gardener. We make great use of this site when we are planning trips to the allotment.

Fig. 13. The home page of iGarden, an internet gardening magazine and portal site.

Internet Directory for Botany
http://www.botany.net/IDB/idb2.html
This Canadian site contains a large number of links to topics such as: arboreta and botanical gardens, botanical societies, international botanical organisations, biologists' addresses, botanical museums, herbaria, natural history museums, checklists and floras, taxonomical databases, vegetation, conservation and threatened plants. You can find out about economic botany, ethnobotany, gardening, images, journals, book, literature databases, and publishers. There are link collections, resource guides, listservers and newsgroups, guides to lower plants and fungi, paleobotany, palynology, pollen, software, and university departments.

Internet Garden
http://www.internetgarden.co.uk
The Internet Garden has been online for about two years, and contains a substantial number of well-organised links. It has been designed to provide a clean and simple interface, free of large image files, and with easy navigational controls. It is constantly in search of new and interesting links, so if you want to suggest a web site to add, get in touch. Well worth a look.

Searching for information..

Organic Gardeners' Web
http://www.geocities.com/RainForest/8810/ogweb.html
This page contains some links to the personal pages of organic gardeners.
The idea is that organic gardeners can find each other and share ideas.

Plant Press
http://www.plantpress.com
The Plant Press publishes gardening, botanical and scientific information on CD-rom, in books and on the web. Its main product is *The Plant
Finder Reference Library* CD-rom, a collection of databases for gardeners, horticultural professionals and botanists on CD-rom for Windows
PCs. This is published as *The RHS Plant Finder* CD-rom in conjunction
with the Royal Horticultural Society and Dorling Kindersley.

Plants Magazine
http://www.plants-magazine.com/index.html
This is the web site of *Plants* magazine, edited by Dirk van der Werff. *Plants*
is a quarterly subscription-only magazine based in north-east England.
There are some useful links to nurseries around the UK and USA.

Royal Horticultural Society
http://www.rhs.org.uk/Around/links.asp
The RHS is Britain's largest gardening organisation. The site is easy to
navigate around and from the home page you can search the RHS database to find books, plants and products. The sites listed and linked here
are divided by subject into organisations, books and bookshops, colleges, gardens, individual plants and genera, societies, and magazine
(general interest) sites. This is an essential bookmark for gardeners.

Virtual Garden
http://vg.com
This is a very substantial and useful site. 'It is created by gardeners, for
gardeners. It is the place to find the inspiration and information you'll
need to help you grow your garden. You can search the Time-Life Plant
Encyclopaedia, interact with other cyber-gardeners, gather helpful hints
for your zone, and explore the world of gardening online.' Dating back to
1994, VG is one of the oldest gardening portals on the web.

Which?Online – Gardening
http://www.which.net/gardening/contents.html
This web site of the Consumers Association contains a whole range of
products, advice, trials, tests, tips, news and ideas to help you get the
most from your garden. It gives quick access to hundreds of useful gardening fact sheets and reports. Registration is required for access to
parts of the site.

Yahoo! UK Gardening
http://uk.dir.yahoo.com/Recreation/Home_and_Garden/Gardening
Don't forget to check out the UK gardening area of the mighty Yahoo!
internet directory.

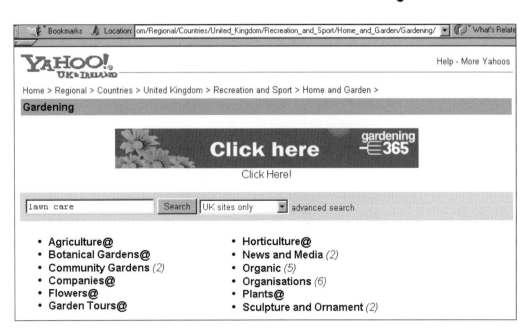

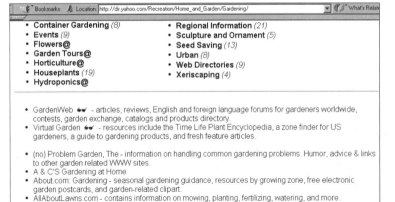

Using the internet directory and search engine Yahoo! to explore gardening web sites.

2 Gardening discussion forums

In this chapter we will explore:

▶ *discussion forums on the internet*

▶ *guidelines on using discussion forums*

▶ *joining an internet mailing list*

▶ *general sources of mailing lists*

▶ *sources of gardening mailing lists*

▶ *a selection of gardening mailing lists*

▶ *bulletin board services (BBS) for gardeners*

▶ *newsgroups (Usenet) for gardeners*

. . . .

Discussion forums on the internet

With the internet, you can potentially communicate with thousands if not millions of fellow gardeners. They could be living around the corner, or in almost any part of the world. This communication takes place through four very popular but distinct aspects of the internet:

1. email
2. mailing lists
3. bulletin boards
4. newsgroups

These last three are known as 'discussion forums'. This chapter introduces what are they and how to use them. The great thing about discussion forums is that they enable you to get in touch with so many people, many of whom have great expertise and are quite willing to share it. This reflects the spirit of community that has been such a powerful force in the internet since its early days, and to a large extent remains so.

Guidelines on using discussion forums

Netiquette
There is an informal but established code of practice on the internet called 'netiquette'. Essentially this comes down to showing good manners and respect to other people on the net. For example, if you were to email every member of a group – perhaps hundreds of people - that you are changing email addresses, it could annoy a great number of people. Equally, there is little point in sending such a message to a computer that is simply programmed to add or remove names from a list.

Commercial messages
If you are in the business of selling gardening products or services, keep in mind that it is considered bad manners to place advertisements or to

try and sell things in discussion forums. If you have some kind of gardening or horticultural business, you might like to look at another title in the Internet Handbooks series, *Marketing Your Business on the Internet*, for guidance on the best ways of using the internet for business.

Spam – junk mail on the internet
Spam is the trade name of the well-known luncheon meat that was popular in the 1960s and immortalised by the Monty Python team. It is also the term widely used on the internet for unwanted email. Certain bulk email companies send out huge amounts of junk email. Unfortunately these messages cost the recipients money, because of the time taken to download them into their 'inbox'. If you upset the members of a mailing list or newsgroup by bombarding them with irrelevant or commercial messages, you may well receive angry emails in return.

Joining an internet mailing list

In internet parlance, a mailing list is a forum where members can distribute messages by email to the members of the forum. All the members – 'subscribers' – can read the messages posted. There are two types of lists, discussion and announcement:

1. Discussion lists allow exchange between list members.
2. Announcement lists are one-way only and used to distribute information such as news or humour.

There are more than 100,000 different mailing lists on the internet, including quite a few for gardeners. Good places to look for specific mailing lists are the web sites of Liszt and Mailbase (see below).

The term mailing list often frightens newcomers to the internet. They think they are about to be swamped with information from unwanted sources. This is not the case. A 'mailing list' on the internet is a specific concept. It means an electronic forum where people with shared interests can exchange information. This exchange takes place by email. A better name might be 'emailing list', but 'mailing list' is the established phrase.

How mailing lists work
Usually, the mailing lists are maintained automatically by computers called listservs. To subscribe (or unsubscribe) all you need to do is send an email to the listserv, and the computer does the rest. It notes your email address, sends you copies of messages posted by fellow subscribers, and distributes any messages that you send to it. Mailing list technology is based on various list server software programs such as Majordomo, Listserv, ListProc and Lyris.

It is important to distinguish between the list administrator – the listserv – and the individuals who actually subscribe to the mailing list. The listserv is simply a computer that automatically maintains the details of the subscribers; the subscribers are of course real people. The people who subscribe to the list will be less than pleased if you bother them with your subscription or other details that you should have addressed to the listserv.

How to subscribe to a mailing list
Subscribing to a mailing list is usually quite easy. Normally you just send an email to the listserv, with the message SUBSCRIBE in the subject line. The listserv recognises this command, and automatically adds you to the mailing list.

▶ Do not use your web-based browser. Use your email program to send your subscription message.

Make sure you type the listserv address exactly as it is shown. Usually, email addresses are written in lower case. Marks like this _ are important; do not ignore them. This mark is called an 'underscore'. Where you come across it, it is a fundamental part of the email address. The email won't arrive unless you include it. Within about 24 hours you should get a response to your request for a subscription. Again, this response will be generated automatically. Don't reply directly to that email address, to send messages to the list.

If you are not sure what to do, email the listserv but leave the subject line blank. Type the word HELP in the body of the text. This should generate a response that explains how to subscribe to the mailing list. The automatic mailing should also tell you how to UNSUBSCRIBE to the group, should you want to leave it.

Some of these mailing lists generate a lot of response. If you subscribe, you will usually receive a copy of all of the messages posted to the group. This is fine, if you can retrieve your mail every day, but if you go away for a week or two you may find your mailbox overflowing. Some of the bigger mailing lists generate hundreds of messages every day. Many are expanding fast as the internet itself grows.

If you intend to go away for while, visit your internet service provider's web site. This should explain how you can redirect your email, or even how to automatically send a message saying that you are not available to answer mail. We have used such a service ourselves and it works well.

Mailing list addresses
Mailing lists have a different type of address from web pages. A mailing list address usually begin with the term 'listserv' followed by the 'at' symbol, @. Web sites on the other hand always begin with the code http:// often followed by www. If you want to take part in mailing lists, you need an email facility. However, if you want to access the world wide web and visit web sites, you will need a browser such as Internet Explorer or Netscape Navigator. (Your browser will almost certainly include an email package as part of the bundle – see Appendix.)

There are upwards of 100,000 mailing lists and they are all subject-related. This means that you can find mailing lists for many special interests in gardening. You will receive email that will relate to the subject on the list, but as people get to know each other, in their online persona, you may find that they sometimes go off subject. This is part of the nature of online communication, in the same way as people often digress in real life.

▶ *Tip* – If you receive unwanted email from a mailing list, reply and type the word REMOVE in the subject line. This should do the trick.

General sources of mailing lists

This section details some of the best-known web sites where you can seek out internet mailing lists. The top names include Liszt, Mailbase, and Reference.Com.

CataList Reference Site
http://www.lsoft.com/lists/listref.html
From this page, you can browse an amazing 38,000 public listserv lists on the internet, search for mailing lists of interest, and get information about listserv host sites. This information is generated automatically and is said to be always up to date (figure 14).

Fig. 14. CataList offers a quick way to find out about more than 27,000 different mailing lists on the internet that you can subscribe to by email.

List of Lists
http://catalog.com/vivian/interest-group-search.html
Here you can search a large directory of special interest group email lists available on the internet. The site includes some subscription instructions if you are not familiar with the procedures for subscribing to mailing lists.

Liszt
http://www.liszt.com
Liszt (note the spelling carefully) offers by far the largest index of mailing lists available on the internet. It covers every conceivable area of interest, with details of more than 90,000 lists in all. It also offers a Usenet news-

Gardening discussion forums...

Fig. 15. Liszt is the biggest and best-known database of internet mailing lists. It also leads quickly to other types of discussion forums including literally tens of thousands of newsgroups and chat rooms.

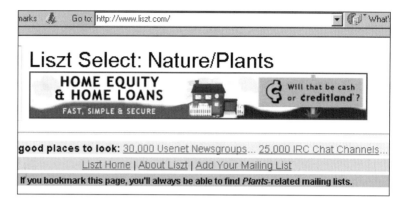

groups directory, and an Internet Relay Chat (IRC) directory. You can obtain a vast amount of information here (figure 15).

MailBase
http://www.mailbase.ac.uk/
Run from the University of Sheffield, MailBase is the best known and largest source of (largely academic) mailing lists in the UK, over 2,000 in all. You can search its database of lists to find the one(s) that interest you, and then subscribe (free) to read and post messages on that particular topic – horticulture, or what you will.

Publicly Accessible Mailing Lists
http://paml.net/
'We're better because we actively keep our mailing list entries up to date. We might not be the biggest, but we personally guarantee that our listings are the most accurate… I've written a few help files that I hope will be useful. For your perusal, there are files that provide pointers to other mailing list compilations and reference sources, and answer the ultimate question: how does one unsubscribe from a mailing list?' (figure 16).

Fig. 16. Publicly Accessible Mailing Lists is another well-known source. This page shows the start of its gardening mailing lists you can subscribe to.

Reference.Com
http://www.reference.com/
Like Liszt, Reference.Com is a top source of information about internet mailing lists.

Tile.Net Lists
http://tile.net/listserv
Tile.Net provides a substantial guide to email discussion, announcements and information lists on the internet.

Sources of gardening mailing lists

Garden Gate Mailing Lists
http://garden-gate.prairienet.org/maillist.htm
To get started with internet mailing lists for gardeners, visit this excellent US site. It will tell you about many gardening-related mailing lists on the internet (figure 17).

The Internet Directory for Botany Listservs
http://www.helsinki.fi/kmus/botnews.html
An internet directory for botany listservs can be found at this web site. You should also find the email addresses to which you send subscription requests, and information to sign on to the list.

▶ *Tip* – If you subscribe to several mailing lists, you may receive an avalanche of messages daily. It might then be a good idea to have email software that sorts by sender. You can then easily keep mailing lists separate from your daily routine mail. A number of mailing lists offer their messages in digest form. This is an option you might wish to pursue, since it limits the amount of daily traffic.

Fig. 17. Garden Gate specialises in providing information about internet mailing lists for gardeners. The site includes some useful guidance on how to subscribe to them and how to use them.

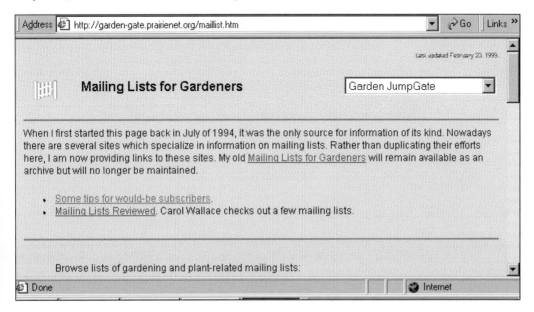

Gardening discussion forums. . . . .

Some internet mailing lists for gardeners

Algardening Mailing List
http://www.alastra.com/internet/paml/groups.A/a1gardening.html
They say: 'This list is for gardeners and florists. A guide to building an incredible successful garden, hundreds of free tips, gardening as a hobby or a profit, Learn how to garden like an expert. Strategies for gardening, home based business. We will subscribe you to our free newsletter. Welcome all!'

Aquatic Plants Mailing List
Discussion in this group seems skewed toward growing plants in tanks. The messages are distributed in digest form. The list administrator compiles all the day's messages and sends them out in one post per day. We enjoy reading this and, as members, recommend it. Send email to: majordomo@actwin.com Message: subscribe aquatic-plants [your email address]. This list asks you to subscribe with your email address, not your name.

Biosph-L Mailing List
The aim here is to discuss the Earth's Biosphere. To subscribe, send email to: listserv@listserv.aol.com In the body of the message put SUBSCRIBE BIOSPH-L Yourfirstname Yourlastname.

Bk2Basics Mailing List
listserv@drcoffsite.com
This is a bit like an American version of *The Good Life*. They talk about issues 'related to return to basic ways of living and achieving happiness. It is a discussion group for people who wish to learn the know-how of the good-ol'-days for future living survival skills. We are interested in maintaining our self-reliance and independence in the present-day and future. Topics may include living off the land, medical self care, how to

Fig. 18. Composter, an example of a Bulletin Board Service (BBS).

grow and use herbs as medicinal plant foods, building community, home schooling, environmental restoration, low input sustainable agriculture, collective gardening techniques, making rather than purchasing products. Subscription message: 'SUBSCRIBE BK2BASICS your name'.

Compost Mailing List
listproc@listproc.wsu.edu
http://www.composter.com/newsgroups.html
This speaks for itself, but remember that US compost conditions are different to UK conditions. *Subscription message:* 'SUBSCRIBE COMPOST your name' or 'JOIN COMPOST your name'. See figure 18.

Dev-Habitat Mailing List
dev-habitat-request@ihnet.it
Dev-Habitat aims to discuss habitat, especially housing, architecture and planning in developing countries. To subscribe, send an email to the address above and write in the body of the message: 'join dev-habitat'.

Ecolog-L Mailing List
listserv@umdd.umd.edu
This is a moderated listserv list aimed at members of the Ecological Society of America. It allows people with a common interest in ecology and related fields to communicate via email. Subscription is free to all and not restricted to ESA members. To subscribe send email to the address above. In the body of your message, put 'SUB Ecolog-L Firstname Lastname'.

Ethology Mailing List
listserv@searn.sunet.se
This is an unmoderated mailing list set up to discuss animal behaviour and behavioural ecology. To subscribe, send email to the address above. In the body of the message, put 'subscribe ETHOLOGY Firstname Lastname'.

Garden UK Mailing List
http://www.garden-uk.org.uk
In researching this book, we also came across Garden UK. This is a delight. We have subscribed to the list ourselves and found it very friendly. We have suddenly found ourselves with a big group of cyber friends who daily exchange information about the garden. The service is run by Louise King. Highly recommended.

Gardens Mailing List
To subscribe, send message to: listserv@ukcc.uky.edu The body of the message should say: subscribe gardens *your name*.

Green-Travel Mailing List
This is a moderated list that concentrates on sharing information about culturally and environmentally responsible, or sustainable, travel and tourism worldwide. To subscribe, send a message to: majordomo@ig-

c.apc.org The body of your message should say: subscribe green-travel

Groundwater Mailing List
http://www.groundwater.com
Groundwater aims to promote the dissemination of information and ideas about groundwater science. To subscribe, send email to: majordomo@ias.champlain.edu In the body of the message put 'subscribe GROUNDWATER'.

Horticulture Mailing List
listserv@vtvm1.cc.vt.edu
To subscribe, send message to the address above. In the body of your message write: 'subscribe hort-l *your name*'.

Hot Peppers Mailing List
listserv@ucdmc.ucdavis.edu
We are told that the list contains some great information about growing peppers. We have not joined it ourselves, so if you join please let us know how it goes. Contact Graham at grahamlawlor@internet-handbooks.co.uk. To join this list, send an email to the address above. Message: 'subscribe chile-heads [your name]'.

Irises Mailing List
listserv@rt66.com
Many breeders and experts take part in this list, so it has a great deal of expertise to offer. However, beginners are welcomed, too. Sometimes there are opportunities for a plant swap. This is a great way to try new varieties. Traffic is fairly heavy, so you may receive about 50 posts a day. Send email to the address above, putting 'subscribe iris-l [your name]' in the message.

Master Gardening Mailing List
To subscribe, send a message to: listproc@listproc.wsu.edu In the body of the message write: subscribe mgarden *your name*.

Organic Gardening Mailing List
listserv@lsv.uky.edu
This list is for gardeners who want to garden without chemicals and want to create habitats in which wildlife can thrive. You can expect about 40 mailings per week. Send an email to the address above, and write 'subscribe ogl' [your name]' in the message area of the email.

Restoration Ecology Mailing List
gadion@macc.wisc.edu

Soil-Chem mailing list
listproc@soils.umn.edu
This is another soils list. To subscribe, send email to the adress above. In the body of the message put 'SUBSCRIBE SOIL-CHEM firstname lastname'.

Soils-1 mailing list
listserv@unl.edu
This is a mailing list dedicated to soils. To subscribe, send an email to the address above. In the body of your message put 'sub soils-l firstname lastname'.

Tree City Urban Forestry Mailing List
majordomo@dainet.de
To subscribe, send a message to the address above, with no subject line. In the body, without quotation, put: 'subscribe urban-forestry *your electronic address* *your name*'.

Waste Mailing List
To subscribe, send a message to: majordomo@cedar.univie.ac.at The body should say: 'subscribe waste your@email.address'. To unsubscribe, the body should say: 'unsubscribe waste yourname@email address'.

Bulletin Board Services

Bulletin board services (BBS) are electronic notice boards. Here, you can read and place notices, just as you would stick messages on a club notice board. Bulletin boards enable people with shared interests to contact each other. They were more popular when the internet was only used by research and military institutions, and before we had online services like CompuServe and AOL. Since they are based on people with a common interest, they often contain useful files which people accessing the bulletin board can download.

The negative side of bulletin boards is that they lack the immediacy of personal contact. They are less popular than once they were, since there are better alternatives in the form of newsgroups, mailing lists, internet relay chat (IRC), and member forums run by the various internet service providers.

The Directory
http://www.thedirectory.org
This site makes an excellent starting point to find out more about BBS. It offers a substantial and worldwide listing of bulletin board systems. It describes itself as 'the world's largest bulletin board system information web site.' There is plenty of practical guidance for users, and links to thousands of actual BBS networks.

What are newsgroups?

Newsgroups are nothing to do with news from television, radio or newspapers. They are a specific and well-established internet concept, completely free, and extremely popular. There are 80,000-plus newsgroups, collectively referred to as Usenet. Each newsgroup is a collection of messages, usually unedited and unchecked by anyone ('unmoderated'). The ever-growing newsgroups have been around for much longer than the world wide web and web pages. They are an endless source of information, news, scandal, entertainment, resources and ideas. A million or more messages ('articles') are posted every day. Messages can be read and posted in any newsgroup by anyone including you.

▶ *The difference between mailing lists and newsgroups* – On a newsgroup, you get to see all of the messages but you have to log on and go to the newsgroup to read them. On a mailing list, the messages are automatically sent to you by email.

How are newsgroups organised?
These are the most common newsgroup categories or 'hierarchies':

alt	alternative interests
uk	United Kingdom issues
us	American interests
comp	computers
rec	recreation interests
soc	social concerns
sci	science
talk	chat
biz	business

Newsgroups are not the same as web pages. The information is presented in a much more basic form, much like email. You will not see fancy graphics or designer pages. It will usually be simple text information, presented in a straightforward and often hard-hitting manner.

How to access a newsgroup
Most internet service providers now provide access to newsgroups as part of their service. In other words, they act as your 'news server' and give you some software called a 'news reader'. This enables you to search, read, post and manage messages in the newsgroups they carry.

Fig. 19. Newsgroups. The bottom left part of the screen shows the gardening newsgroups subscribed to by the author of this book, Graham Lawlor. His newsreader software is the ever-popular Outlook Express.

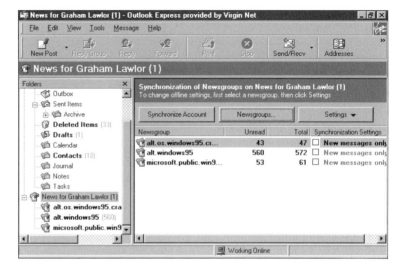

For the vast majority of people using PCs with Windows operating systems, their newsreader will either be Outlook Express (which comes with the browser Internet Explorer), or Messenger (which comes with the browser Netscape Communicator).

Accessing newsgroups with Internet Explorer/Outlook Express
In Outlook Express, choose the Newsgroups option from the Tools menu. Go down the folders column in the left-hand window pane, and you will find an icon for news. See figure 19. You can see that the user has subscribed to a number of newsgroups. He uses these as a way of keeping up to date with technical changes and as a way of sharing experiences and answers that other people may have found.

Click on the Newsgroups button on the main toolbar. This should display a number of newsgroups in a window as in figure 20. If you

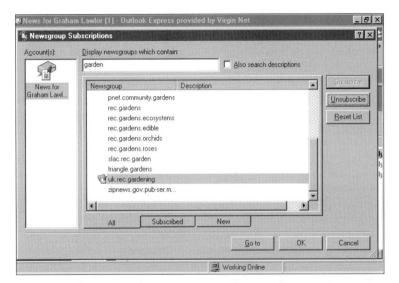

Fig. 20. This screen (Outlook Express again) shows the results of a search for newsgroups whose name includes the word 'garden'. To subscribe to a newsgroup, just highlight its name and click Subscribe on the right-hand side of the screen.

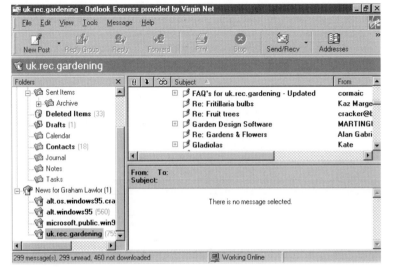

Fig. 21. Using Outlook Express again, Graham has displayed the message headers for a popular newsgroup called uk.rec.gardening. The message headers are displayed in the upper right window pane.

35

Gardening discussion forums...

Fig. 22. To display a
newsgroup message, just
click on the name of the
header, in this case the
line which reads 'welcome
to newcomers'. The
message then appears
below (Outlook Express).

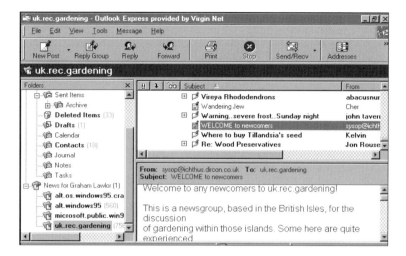

have nothing in this window, you need to connect to the internet in the
usual way, and then wait while all the newsgroups download onto your
computer. (The first time you ever do this, it could take 10 to 20 minutes
for the names of 20 or 30 thousand newsgroups to be loaded onto your
computer – be patient until the process is completed. You won't need to
do it again.)

As you can see, the user has typed in the word 'garden' at the top of
the page and then has clicked on 'uk.rec.gardening'. This is a very friendly
group and very welcoming. Figure 21 shows some of the messages that
were on the newsgroup, on the day we logged on. Figure 22 shows a
welcoming message to any new member. Don't be afraid to join in; it's
great fun, and you could learn all kinds of new things about gardening.

Accessing newsgroups with Netscape Messenger
On the main Netscape Communicator toolbar, click Communicator, then
Newsgroups (figure 23). Once you have done this, as with Outlook
Express, the name of your news server (e.g. news.virgin.net) will
appear in the left-hand pane, along with the names of any newsgroups
you have subscribed to (figure 24). Click on the name of a newsgroup to
display all its message headers in the top right-hand pane. Next, click on
any header to display the actual message ('article') in the bottom right-
hand pane.

Fig. 23. Finding News-
groups in Netscape 4.
Click on Communicator,
then Newsgroups.

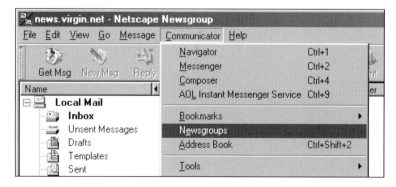

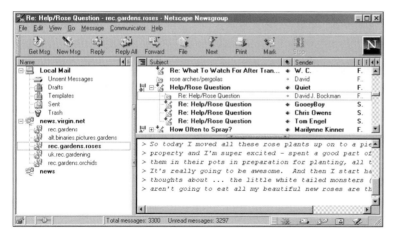

Fig. 24. In Netscape, as in Outlook Express, the left-hand window pane shows the news server (news.virgin.net in this case) and the newsgroups which have been subscribed to, such as rec.gardens.roses.

If no newsgroups have been selected, right-click on the name of your news server (in figure 24 it is news.virgin.net), then click Subscribe to Newsgroups. A list of all newsgroups offered by your news server will appear in a box which opens up. As with Outlook Express, the first time you ever do this, it could take 10 to 20 minutes for the names of tens of thousands of newsgroups to be loaded onto your computer – be patient until the process is completed. You won't need to do it again. Once the complete list of newsgroups has been successfully down-loaded, just click on the name of any one you wish to open. Alternatively, click the Search tab at the top, and type in 'gardening' or other keyword(s).

Newsgroups for gardeners

Now, here are some examples of actual Usenet newsgroups, where people read and post messages about gardening topics. To access any such group, you can just type the address exactly as shown below into your browser's address box, in other words the name of the newsgroup, prefixed by 'news:'. Your newsreader (typically Outlook or Messenger) will then open, and you will see the name of the newsgroup in the pane on the left of the screen. Click on the newsgroup name, and the message headers (single line descriptions) in the newsgroup should then appear in the top right-hand pane on your screen. Click on any header, and the message will be displayed in the bottom right-hand pane.

news:alt.agriculture.fruit
news:alt.agriculture.misc
news:alt.sustainable agriculture
news:rec.gardens
news:rec.gardens.ecosystems
news:rec.gardens.edidle
news:rec.gardens.gardening
news:rec.gardens.orchids
news:rec.gardens.roses
news:talk.environment

Gardening discussion forums...

news:triangle.gardens
news.uk.environment
news:uk.rec.gardening

What about undesirable material?
Some unscrupulous people use newsgroups for displaying pornography or peddling spurious get-rich-quick schemes. Even an innocent newsgroup on gardening may occasionally contain offensive material. Look carefully at the title line ('header') of a message before opening and reading it. If the header contains a suggestive comment, just ignore it.
It is important to recognise that a newsgroup does not exist in a specific geographical location. The newsgroups are maintained by thousands of 'news servers' all over the world. These are computers whose sole function is to automatically and instantly share all posted messages with all other news servers.

Supervising children's access to newsgroups
If you have children in the house, it would be sensible to monitor their use of newsgroups, even when they are exploring gardening or other apparently innocuous newsgroups. A good plan is to place the computer in an area of the home that the whole family uses. It is not a good idea for children to have computers in their own rooms, where their internet use cannot be monitored.

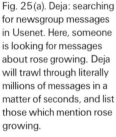

Fig. 25(a). Deja: searching for newsgroup messages in Usenet. Here, someone is looking for messages about rose growing. Deja will trawl through literally millions of messages in a matter of seconds, and list those which mention rose growing.

Some internet service providers provide parental tools that can stop children accessing undesirable material. Contact your ISP for more advice on this matter. You can also obtain software packages that filter undesirable material. NetNanny and CyberSitter are two well-known examples. Contact your local computer store for more about this, or see Graham Jones' paperback, *Protecting Children on the Internet*, in the Internet Handbooks series.

Deja

http://www.deja.com/usenet/

If you have a query, such as 'rose growing', you can use this popular site to instantly search tens of thousands of newsgroups (figure 25). Deja will then list every message which mentions rose growing. Deja was founded in 1995 as the first web site dedicated exclusively to online discussion, and capable of searching and archiving Usenet newsgroups. With more than six million page views a day, it offers access to over 45,000 news-groups. Not surprisingly, it is one of the web's most visited sites. More than a million people have registered (free) to take advantage of its expanding range of information and community services.

In the next chapter, we introduce some of the specialist gardening societies and interest groups with web pages on the internet.

▶ *Tip* – If you would like to find out more about internet mailing lists, newsgroups and bulletin board services and how they work, take a look at *Discussion Forums on the Internet* by Kye Valongo in the Internet Handbooks series.

Fig. 25(b). This shows the result for a search for messages about rose-growing, using Deja. It has found 700 messages, in a newsgroup called rec.gardens.roses. To read a particular message, just click on the appropriate line.

| | Bookmarks | Go to: ww.deja.com]/dnquery.xp?DBS=1&svcclass=dnserver&QRY=rose+growing |

Results for: "rose growing"   **MY** Save this Search

Discussion Forums

　　　　>> rec.gardens.roses

Messages
1-25 of 700 matches   Page 1 of 28 Next >>

Date ▼	Subject ▼	Forum ▼	Author ▼
07/05/2000	Rose identification	**rec.gardens.roses**	Stan Wright
07/05/2000	Re: Rose identification	**rec.gardens.roses**	Gayle or Stan
07/05/2000	Re: Rose identification	**rec.gardens.roses**	Diana Choi
06/29/2000	Re: What did I end up with?	**rec.gardens.roses**	Bob Bauer
06/27/2000	Rose Politics	**rec.gardens.roses**	Bob Bauer
07/06/2000	Can't we all get along?	**rec.gardens.roses**	Peacemaker
07/05/2000	Re: Rose identification	**rec.gardens.roses**	Angelique
07/01/2000	Re: Does anyone know about a	**rec.gardens.roses**	Baldo Villegas
06/27/2000	Re: Need a Rose Shrub to rep	**rec.gardens.roses**	Propp
06/26/2000	Re: Does anyone know about a	**rec.gardens.roses**	John Grunden
06/16/2000	Re: Rose DOT com name sugges	**rec.gardens.roses**	Silvirado
07/06/2000	Re: Can't we all get along?	**rec.gardens.roses**	Angelique

3 Specialist societies

In this chapter we will explore:

▶ *general information*

▶ *horticultural societies*

▶ *trade associations*

▶ *public bodies*

▶ *individual plant families and genera*

▶ *kitchen and allotment gardening*

General information

There are innumerable sites of interest to gardeners with special interests. These range from cactus to zinnias, dahlias to sweet peas, allotments to organic gardening, and a great deal more. If you are interested in a particular plant or type of gardening there's bound to be something for you online. The specialist society sites often give you a lot of free information, whilst many of the interest groups are in the form of clubs that you can join to exchange information, hints, tips, or just gossip if you want.

Backyard Gardener (US)
http://backyardgardener.com
This is a huge American site with page after page of information, photographs, cultural instructions and links with other associated sites (figure 26). Some of the trans-Atlantic language may be unfamiliar, and some of the products may not yet be available in the UK. Vegetable seeds on

Fig. 26. Backyard Gardener is packed with useful information, tips and gardening links.

paper strips have only recently been introduced here and are available in a limited number of varieties from only a few seed merchants. No doubt this will change if the technique becomes popular with gardeners. However, whatever information you want on any aspect of gardening, this site is a must.

Discovering Annuals

http://www.discoveringannuals.com
Moving from perennials to annuals, this is a site from Graham Rice, gardening correspondent of the *London Evening Standard*. It is based on a book of the same name. The site and the book are devoted to annuals of all kinds: hardy annuals, half-hardy annuals, biennials and seed raised bedding plants (figure 27).

Fig. 27. The Discovering Annuals web site is based on a book of the same name, written by Graham Rice.

Internet Directory for Botany

http://www.botany.net/IDB/index.html
The Internet Directory of Botany is an authoritative index to botanical information available on the internet - a vast compilation of sources which you can explore by subject, or alphabetically.

Horticultural societies

Alpine Garden Society

http://www.alpinegardensoc.demon.co.uk
Founded in 1929, the Society has an international membership of over

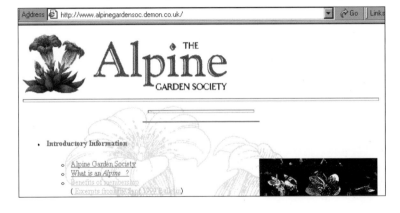

Fig. 28. The Alpine Garden Society has been enterprising in using the internet to disseminate information about alpines, and news about its various activities and shows.

Specialist societies ....

13,000 including several UK local groups (figure 28). It seeks to promote interest in all aspects of alpine plants, both in their natural habitats and in cultivation. The term alpine refers to any plant that grows above the tree line in mountainous areas. In gardening terms it refers to any small hardy plant or bulb that is largely perennial. Alpines can be grown in natural habitats such as woodlands and in man-made habitats such as rockeries, troughs, scree beds, pots and containers and in alpine houses. There is an impressive list of publications available by mail order. Membership details are shown on the site.

Iris Growing Info

Iris Photos

Iris Classifications

AIS Awards

100 Most Popular Iris

AIS Bulletin Excerpts

Email Lists & Chat Ni

AIS Storefront

American Iris Society
http://www.irises.org
If it's irises you are interested in then the AIS web site may be worth a visit. It explains how to grow them and the conditions they need. 'Iris-talk' is an open email list where you can get involved in discussing irises and iris related topics with other enthusiasts. You can also read interesting excerpts from past issues of the Society's magazine. There are photographs of award winning irises and links to other iris-related sites. Overseas membership starts at $23.

American Rhododendron Society
http://www.rhododendron.org
This attractively presented and substantial web site offers information and connectivity to the expanding world of rhododendron and azalea horticulture. It has more than 1,000 plants in its online database.

Arboricultural Association
http://www.trees.org.uk
The AA is a charitable organisation based in the UK with over 2,000 members dedicated to conserving, enhancing and protecting Britain's heritage of amenity trees for the enjoyment and benefit of this and future generations. This useful site includes detailed lists of all the Association's approved contractors and consultants, and a set of links to sites of related interest.

Botanic Gardens Conservation International
http://www.bgci.org.uk
This is an international conservation organisation based at the Royal Botanical Gardens, Kew. It provides technical guidance, data and support for botanic gardens in almost 100 countries worldwide. It has a wide range of activities, meetings, workshops, congresses and training courses from Poland to China, Colombia, Mexico and Russia.

Botanical Society of the British Isles
http://members.aol.com/bsbihgs
The BSBI was founded in 1836 and has played a central role in the botanical community for 160 years. It offers its members, whether beginners or seasoned professionals, services and a forum for the exchange of ideas and information. The web site includes links to other sites of botanic interest.

Botanical Society of Scotland
http://www.rbge.org.uk/bss
Founded in 1836, the Society exists to promote the study of plants and to exchange botanical knowledge between members. It is the only British botanical society with a keen interest in both flowering and non-flowering plants (e.g. algae, mosses, ferns, and fungi). It also has an active alpine flora section. It holds regular meetings in Glasgow, Aberdeen, Dundee, St Andrews, Inverness, and Edinburgh.

British & European Geranium Society
http://www.fitzjohn.linkuk.co.uk
Another good site for pelargoniums and geraniums is BEGS, formed in 1970. It contains a great deal of cultural information and details of the various types of geraniums and pelargoniums including ivy, zonal, regal, scented and angel. The site includes membership details, information about geranium care, shows, nurseries, plenty of useful links and more.

British Cactus & Succulent Society
http://www.cactus-mall.com/bcss
Membership of the BCSS stands at about 3,800 and includes the whole spectrum of gardenings from novice window-sill growers to experts. The Society has just under 100 branches in the UK, which organise an active programme of events every year.

British Fuchsia Society
http://www.ndirect.co.uk/∼martync/bfspage.htm
This is a basic information site which sets out details of local events around the UK. There are hyperlinks to the web sites of some of its local affiliated groups.

Carnivorous Plant Society (USA)
http://www.sarracenia.com
Here you can learn about the ecology, cultivation, conservation, and taxonomy of carnivorous plants. The large number of questions and answers are presented in cooperation with the International Carnivorous Plant Society.

Cyclamen Society
http://www.cyclamen.org
This is a well-stocked site packed with information and illustrations about cyclamen species (figure 29). It includes details of species, cultivation, books and expeditions. The society has a useful site if you are interested in growing this plant either in pots for the home, or the hardy type in the garden. There are plenty of tips on how to cultivate these Mediterranean plants and to propagate them successfully from corms and from seed. Useful links will tell you where you can obtain plants, corms and seed. If you join the society you can obtain seed direct from them.

Specialist societies ....

Fig. 29. The Cyclamen Society is another very useful site devoted to one particular plant genus.

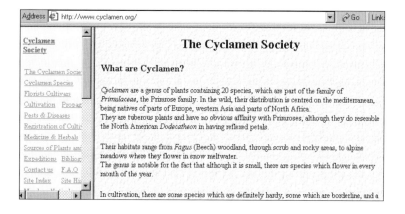

Delphinium Society
http://www.delphinium.demon.co.uk
If you are a delphinium junkie, then the Delphinium Society site is certainly worth a visit (figure 30). Here you will find details of the Society's activities and a useful picture gallery of varieties and hybrids. Unfortunately there is little in the way of cultural information.

Fig. 30. The home page of the Delphinium Society web site. There are plenty of things to look up and take part in here.

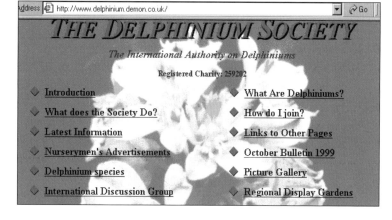

Gardeners' Royal Benevolent Society
jan@gardeners-grbs.demon.co.uk
This is the email contact address of the national charity which supports disabled and retired professional gardeners and horticulturalists.

Heather Society
http://www.users.zetnet.co.uk/heather
Promotes and encourages interest in heathers. Its site includes guidance on the cultivation of heathers.

Hebe Society
http://www.gwynfryn.demon.co.uk/hebesoc/index.htm
http://www.maes-glas.freeserve.co.uk/hebesoc
Encourages the growing, conservation and improvement of hebes.

International Carnivorous Plant Society (US)
http://www.carnivorousplants.org
'If you have questions about these bizarre bloodthirsty plants, take a look at our comprehensive FAQ (frequently asked questions) site where we try to answer just about every carnivorous plant-related question we could think of!'

Institute of Horticulture
http://www.horticulture.demon.co.uk/
The IOH is the authoritative organisation representing all those professionally engaged in horticulture in the UK and Ireland. Its membership comprises, and represents, all those involved in the management, growing and marketing of all edible and decorative horticultural crops, and the research, education and consultancy concerned with them. It also includes those concerned with botanic gardens and landscaping, and horticulture within leisure industries and those in associated supply industries.

Japanese Garden Society in the UK
http://www.camera.u-net.com/gardens/japanese/jgs/jgs.htm
Membership of the JGS brings together amateurs and professionals, garden lovers and garden constructors. The Society meets at various UK locations throughout the year. Meetings range from lectures to three-day events with exhibits. Overseas tours, especially to Japan, are also organised. The site includes a clickable map of Japanese-style gardens open to the public in the UK and Ireland and the basics of Japanese garden styles.

Lakeland Horticultural Society
http://www.cragview.demon.co.uk
The LHS is a registered charity founded in 1969 to 'promote and develop the science, practice and art of horticulture, particularly with regard to conditions prevailing in the Lake District'. The gardens are located in the grounds of Holehird Mansion near Windermere. The site gives some details of plants, national collections, and links to other web sites.

Linnean Society of London
http://www.linnean.org.uk
Based in London, this old-established body is a living forum for biology, dedicated to the science of natural history in all its branches. You can find out about how to visit the Society, who's who, its professional scientific and membership journals, its collections of flora and fauna, its library and print collections, an email announcement service for conferences, events and publications, and membership details.

Magnolia Society (US)
http://www.tallahassee.net/~magnolia
TMS is a USA-based international non-profit plant society founded in 1963 for the purpose of promoting education and exchange of information on these beautiful plants.

Specialist societies ....

Plant America (US)
http://www.plantamerica.org
This is a good US site with access to thousands of photographs of plants.

Royal Horticultural Society
http://www.rhs.org.uk
The RHS is Britain's largest gardening organisation. The site is easy to navigate around and from the Home Page you can search the RHS database to find books, plants and products. The plant finder facility is very useful if you are looking for a supplier in your area of a particular plant, or by mail order. One very interesting part of the site is the details of current RHS plant trials taking place at Wisley, and what trials are planned for the future. There are also guidelines on conservation and the environment and details of horticultural courses and qualifications. Many keen amateur gardeners take the RHS General Certificate because it provides a good basic grounding in horticulture without being too academic. The site explains where you can study for this. There are plenty of benefits if you decide to become an RHS member, such as free entry to many of its shows and to the RHS gardens at Wisley and to Rosemoor in Devon.

Fig. 31. The web site of the Royal Horticultural Society – 'gateway to gardening' – contains a large amount of useful information and is probably an essential bookmark.

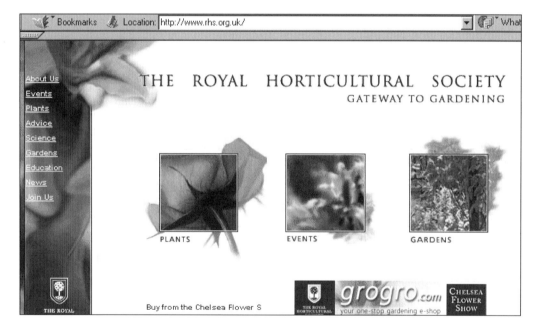

Royal National Rose Society
http://www.roses.co.uk
Another plant that no garden should be without is the best loved of all garden plants, the rose. Rose lovers are catered for by the RNRS which claims to be the oldest and largest specialist plant society. If you need any information about growing roses or just want a few planting ideas, then this site is for you. Gone are the days of massed plantings of roses in beds. Today you can find roses suitable for hanging baskets, pots, tubs,

patio containers of all sorts, and as ground cover, as well as the more traditional bedding varieties, not forgetting the climbers and ramblers.

World Federation of Rose Societies
http://www.worldrose.org
This is an association of the national rose societies of 37 countries, and a gateway to information about roses and rose-growing around the world.

Public bodies

Countryside Agency
http://www.countryside.gov.uk
This is a newly-formed statutory body dedicated to the preservation of the English countryside. Its web site contains information and links on such topics as rights of way, training and research, national parks, rural development areas, village shops and similar matters.

English Heritage
http://www.english-heritage.org.uk
This is a public body responsible for protecting the nation's historic environment.

English Nature
http://www.english-nature.org.uk
English Nature is the government agency that champions the conservation of wildlife and natural features throughout England. It is responsible for safeguarding the nation's variety of wild plants and animals, and its natural features. The site includes publications with online ordering, and maps from the Geographic Information Unit, together with news and a search facility.

Forestry Commission
http://www.forestry.gov.uk
You are invited to 'take a stroll through the site to find out more about the country's forests and what the Forestry Commission is doing to protect and expand them.' There are links to recreation, education, the forestry industry, grants and licences, and forest research.

Horticulture Research International
http://www.hri.ac.uk
HRI is a UK research institute, and the single largest team of horticultural research and development scientists in the world. Its customers include UK research councils, government departments, the EC, overseas agencies, growers and grower-funded levy bodies. HortiTech is its commercial and marketing arm.

International Tree Foundation
http://www.eclipse.co.uk/jns
The society is dedicated to the planting, care and preservation of trees throughout the world. This new site details its various projects. Links to international sites are planned for the future.

Specialist societies ....

Ministry of Agriculture, Fisheries and Food (MAFF)
http://www.maff.gov.uk
This web site explains how MAFF seeks to improve the economic perfor-
mance of the agriculture, fishing and food industries, especially in the
expanding markets of Europe and the wider world. At the same time it
aims to protect our health and conserve the natural environment.

UK Climate

About us

Education

Services

Research

Links

Enquiries

News

Search

MetWEB

The Meteorological ('Met') Office
http://www.meto.govt.uk
This substantial and clearly designed site offers up-to-date weather
information from the UK, and links to weather around the world by
means of a clickable world map. Weather warnings are occasionally
issued when severe weather is expected to cause disruption to travel
(or to gardeners!).

Museum of Garden History
http://www.compulink.co.uk/ ~ museumgh
The world's first Museum of Garden History is at the restored church of
St Mary-at-Lambeth next to Lambeth Palace, the London residence of
the Archbishop of Canterbury. Its web pages give you a flavour of what
to expect from a visit, tell you about its programmes of activities and
lectures, and provide links to other internet sites of interest.

National Council for the Conservation of Plants and Gardens
http://www.nccpg.org.uk
Based at Wisley Gardens, the Council started the National Plant Collections Scheme. This has resulted in more than 600 collections and the
future security of some 50,000 garden plants.

National Gardens Scheme
http://www.ngs.org.uk
Based in Guildford, Surrey, the National Gardens Scheme is a charity
which raises money for nursing and caring charities by opening gardens
of quality and interest to the public. The web site includes a garden-finder,
gardening news, events, garden stories, garden links and similar features.

National Trust
http://www.nationaltrust.org.uk
The National Trust was founded in 1895 to preserve places of historic
interest or natural beauty permanently for the nation to enjoy. The site
contains county by county information on the Trust's many famous
houses, gardens and other properties, together with visitor information.

Natural History Museum
http://www.nhm.ac.uk
The Natural History Museum in west London is the UK's national
museum of natural history, and a centre of scientific excellence in taxonomy and biodiversity. This substantial and well-presented site features a
Botany Department, and there are some helpful links to botanical sites
and gardens.

Trade associations

British Orchid Growers Association
http://www.oncil.demon.co.uk/CSMPage8.htm
This is a trade organisation of commercial orchid nursery owners.

Commercial Horticultural Association
http://www.ukexnet.co.uk/hort/cha
The CHA is the trade association for manufacturers and suppliers of plants, products and services to commercial growers throughout the world. It is based at the National Agricultural Centre, Stoneleigh Park, Kenilworth, Warwickshire. The site can be read in English, French, German and Spanish.

Country Landowners Association
http://www.cla.org.uk
The 50,000 members of the CLA have a common interest in countryside issues. Some members own large farms and estates, others smaller amounts of land, but all share a commitment to rural life. Its members own and manage 60% of the countryside in England and Wales. The site describes the work of the CLA, and features education, links, news, and a Virtual Village.

Virtual Village
Welcome to the CLA Virtual Village.

Click on any part of the village scene to explore.

Looking for something in particular? Use the Search facility or try the Quick Links.

Flowers & Plants Association
http://www.flowers.org.uk
This association is the UK's promotional organisation for cut flowers and indoor plants. It represents the whole floriculture industry. The site includes such features as where to buy flowers and plants, making your cut flowers live longer, arranging for beginners, improving your health with houseplants, jobs in floriculture, and upcoming shows and exhibitions.

Horticultural Trades Association
http://www.martex.co.uk/hta
This is a UK trade organisation, headquartered in Reading, Berkshire. You can search its online directories for garden centres, nurseries, landscapers, retailers, wholesalers and manufacturers. There are links to members' web sites. The site also explains about national garden gift tokens, HTA specialist groups, and its nursery certification scheme.

International Fertiliser Industry Association
http://www.fertilizer.org
Based in Paris, the IFA is a non-profit industrial organisation with around 500 member companies in about 80 countries. The web site includes technical and membership information, forthcoming events, publications, statistics and useful links.

Specialist societies ....

Individual plant families and *genera*

Azalea Works

http://www.theazaleaworks.com

The Azalea Works is an educational and research project devoted to consulting and lecturing, plant research, the development of improved azalea cultivars, and the production and sale of pamphlets and books on azaleas, rhododendron, and related companion plants. This is an introductory site, with links to pages of related interest.

Canna Lily

http://www.farnborough.u-net.com/canna

Here is a site for the lily enthusiast. It is dedicated to the exotic looking canna lily, which is quite easy to grow. Cannas are most often seen as a dot plant in municipal parks and gardens, less often in private gardens - a shame, because their exotic flowers and tall bronze or green foliage are so striking. Although tender perennials, they will grow well in the UK given protection from frost. In sheltered areas of the south they can be left outside during winter if well covered with a mulch of leaves, straw, compost or fleece. In the north or in frost-prone areas the plants can be potted up and brought into a frost-free shed or conservatory. Alternatively, cannas are perfect for growing in pots, but make sure the pots are big enough as they do grow well.

Clematis

Fig. 32. This is a good example of an enthusiast's web site, John Howells on Clematis. If you have some specialist knowledge or enthusiasm, why not create your own gardening web site for others to enjoy and learn from?

http://www.howells98.freeserve.co.uk

Clematis, in all its different forms and varieties, is one of the most popular garden plants, particularly for growing up fences and walls, and for disguising sheds. They are deservedly popular because of their wonderful flowers and relative ease of cultivation. They combine well with roses and will grow almost anywhere. There are various types of clematis and with careful selection you can have clematis in flower from spring through to autumn. A good site to visit is this (figure 32). If you click on publications

| Address | http://www.howells98.freeserve.co.uk/ | ▼ | ⟳ Go | Links |

Howells on Clematis

Welcome to the Howells on Clematis web site. This site lists books, articles and information on clematis by Dr Howells an

Dr John Howells is a former Member of Council of the International Clematis Society and has edited it's publication *Clematis International*. A past Chairman of the British Clematis Society and a former editor of *The Clematis*, he has been elected 'Honorary Member' of the Society and is currently Consultant Editor to its journal. He is the clematis correspondent to *Garden News* and is the author of several horticultural books on clematis.

Dr Howells is responsible for 48 medical books and 300 papers in the international scientific literature. As an international medical authority and former Director of a research institute, he has travelled extensively and been able to acquaint himself with horticultural and botanical institutions world-wide. He cultivates his own garden on a you can read some of his many articles published *in Garden News*. These will give you enough information to get started with clematis. The site has a great deal of interesting information about the clematis, including how to prune them, something that mystifies many gardeners, and not just beginners. There are also details of books about clematis and links with other clematis related sites.

Dowdeswell's Delphiniums
http://www.delphinium.co.nz
One very popular plant − not strictly an annual but sometimes grown as an annual from seed or cutting − is the delphinium. These majestic plants are fairly easy to grow from seed but do require care. Buying young plants from a reputable supplier and taking cuttings is an alternative. This is one of the best delphinium sites we have come across (figure 33). There are plenty of hints and tips about choosing the best plants, where to grow them, how to look after them, as well as growing from seed and cuttings. The picture gallery is excellent. If there's anything you want to know about delphiniums and how to grow them, this New Zealand site is the one to visit.

Fig. 33. Dowdeswell's Delphiniums in another example of the value of the internet in displaying lots of useful related information around one topic.

Hemerocallis
http://www.ofts.com/bill/daylily.html
This site deals with a slightly more exotic plant (figure 34). The site is American and devoted to the hemerocallis, or day lily. The plant is so called because each individual flower only lasts for a single day. But as the plant is very prolific there are always plenty more blooms waiting to

Fig. 34. A web site devoted to the Hemerocallis, or day lily.

open. Easy to grow in a variety of conditions and soils, hemerocallis is a reliable and spectacular plant for summer colour either as a dot plant (or spot plant) or in a mass planting. It can also be grown in pots and containers. Visit the site to find out more about the culture of this beautiful but rather neglected plant. There are plenty of pictures to whet your appetite, and a jazz trio if your speakers are switched on.

Osteospermum
http://www.osteospermum.com
This colourful site dedicated to osteospermums (figure 35). If you are not familiar with these delightful South African daisies, you can find out all about them here, and how to grow and care for them. There is a fine gallery of photographs of varieties, together with details of specialist nurseries that supply them. There are some useful links to other osteospermum sites, and to general gardening sites.

Fig. 35. An Osteospermum web site.

Kitchen and allotment gardening

For gardeners interested in kitchen gardening there are plenty of useful web sites worth a visit. Here are some you might like to explore.

National Society of Allotment and Leisure Gardeners
http://www.nsalg.demon.co.uk
The Society exists to promote local associations, and to assist with registration, model rule books, tenancy agreements, administrative ser-

Fig. 36. The National Society of Allotment and Leisure Gardeners has its own useful web site. This page shows some of the links you can click to obtain more information and contacts in the allotment world.

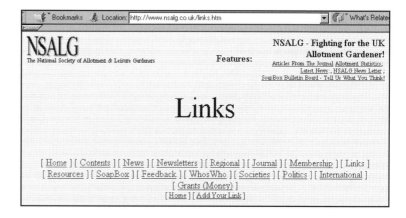

vices, stationery, insurance, legal advice and to protect members interests by lawful means. The web site (figure 36) has links to contents, news, newsletters, regional, journal, membership, links, resources, soapbox, feedback, who's who, societies, politics, international, and grants.

Potatoes Online
http://www.spud.co.uk
Potatoes Online is a site full of technical and statistical information on the cultivation and cooking of potatoes. It is designed for consumers and producers alike, and includes a list of potato varieties.

Wavendon Allotment and Garden Society
http://www.ncare.co.uk/wags
This is an excellent place to explore allotment gardening. The WAGS site is a member of the Allotment and Vegetable Gardening Ring. To see other sites of interest to vegetable gardeners, composters, and people interested in organic produce, you can click on the links provided – there is a whole network of people and organisations out there.

Herbs
Many people never think of growing herbs, yet many are quite straightforward to grow. Even if you live in a flat, you can still grow herbs in pots and enjoy them. It is a delight to have herbs that you can easily go and crop and add to dishes. Here then are a couple of herb sites. It is quite straightforward and great fun to grow herbs, so why not give it a go?

Herb Society
http://www.herbsociety.co.uk
This is the site of the Herb Society, well worth a look (figure 37). Among the features are herbal knowledge: are you satisfied to rest on your

Fig. 37. The web site of the Herb Society.

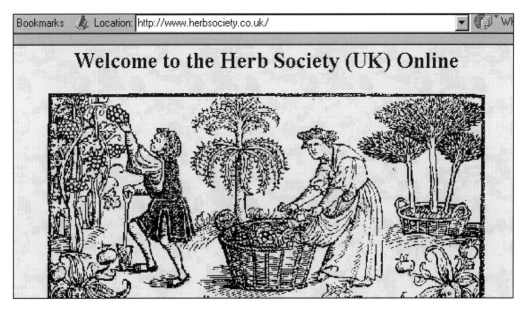

Bookmarks	Location:	http://www.herbsociety.co.uk/

Welcome to the Herb Society (UK) Online

laurels? – and herbal legislation: a summary of new challenges to UK herbal medicine. It also serves as a gateway to lots of other herbal sites around the world.

Whole Herb
http://www.wholeherb.com
Whole Herb is an American site detailing more than 50 herbs. It includes advice on growing, drying, freezing, and recipes for use in food and cosmetics.

4 Gardening health and safety

In this chapter we will explore:

▶ *the ergonomics of gardening*
▶ *ergonomics, disabilities and ageing*
▶ *using electrical tools*
▶ *raised beds for easier gardening*
▶ *gardening as therapy*

. . . .

The ergonomics of gardening

Along the way we will be suggesting certain products to you and telling you where you can buy them. These products will make your gardening easier, and more enjoyable. However, this opinion is not necessarily to be taken as an endorsement of the product, and we have not sought or received any payment from any manufacturer.

Ergonomics is the science of design, in which products are designed to fit people. However, in many ways, people are still expected to fit the products they buy. This is particularly true in the garden. Many of us have tools that were bought years ago, tools that we would have expected to use for life. But are the tools in your garden shed really the best for the job?

If that sounds a silly question, pause and think again. Graham has a back injury from playing sport as a young man. When we went to buy some new garden tools, forks, spades and shovels, we looked at various products and then noticed tools with extended shafts. An extended shaft on a tool makes is easier to dig with. This is a consequence of the torque that is developed, as you dig. In simple terms, the force that you apply in digging, multiplied by the length of the shaft, increases the torque. This is why the digging is made easier.

This means that Graham can now dig in the garden and not suffer the back pain that he has endured for the last twenty years. This is an example of how ergonomics can help you to choose the right tools for the garden. In this chapter we will surf the net to try to show you where suitable products can be obtained.

A sea-change is now taking place in industry and right across the world. The power of the internet means that if you cannot buy the product you want from the garden centre near where you live, you most certainly can from a supplier abroad.

Long tools and ergonomics

Do take some time before buying new tools. It is interesting to spend time in garden centres and DIY stores, and watch how people buy tools. It's amazing to see how many people walk into a store, and buy a product based on price. This is very short-sighted. People will often buy without giving more than a perfunctory glance at the price or the quality of the product.

Gardening health and safety...

When you want a new long tool, for example, you need to have an idea of the length of the shaft that you require. The easiest approach is to stand, with your back straight, and your hands extended, as if you were holding a fork. Then get your companion to measure the distance from your extended hands to the ground. This distance is the length that you need the tool to be. Don't forget, this is not the length of the shaft. It is the length of the shaft and the implement on the end. When you visit a DIY store, take your measure along and measure the implements that they have for sale. If you are tall, you will be amazed at how small some of the tools can be. If you are small or petite, do not assume that long-shafted tools will be too difficult for you. Even someone petite can benefit from using long-shafted tools, since they are easier to dig into the earth.

Buying products over the internet
Many people tell us that they are concerned about the risks of buying over the internet. The fear of the unknown is understandable, but it is a fear you should overcome. Think of all the times when you have quoted your credit-card number. Most people do this without a thought. There have been cases of fraud, but they only make media headlines because they are so rare. In fact thousands of transactions take place daily over the internet, and the vast majority of people are perfectly happy with the outcome.

Demanding quality
Consider the quality of products you are offered. There is no reason to accept inferior goods. If you pay for goods with a credit card, you should find that the credit card company insures the goods. It is worth contacting your credit card company if you are having problems. If the product you have bought is not up to scratch, send it back and demand a refund. Most companies will do their best to help you, but there are some charlatans.

▶ *Credit card shopping* – take a look at a companion title in the Internet Handbooks series, *Using Credit Cards on the Internet* (Graham Jones).

A complaint
We had a situation where we paid for a product with a credit card. The product never arrived. Despite many phone calls we received nothing. We then phoned the credit card company, which was extremely helpful. Within 24 hours it had retrieved our money from the supplier concerned. The credit card company has the power to withdraw merchant status from the offending supplier. That company will no longer be able to trade over the phone or over the internet, because they will no longer be able to accept Visa or Mastercard numbers. This is a real penalty for them.

Another complaint
When we were researching for this book, we came across an old copy of a well-known UK gardening magazine. It contained a letter from a lady who had bought a garden fork. When her husband used the fork, a tine

broke off. When she contacted the supplier, the supplier said the fork was designed for light forking only. This had not been made clear on the packaging. When the lady asked what her husband should use to dig their heavy clay garden, she was recommended to use a pickaxe. This was unacceptable nonsense. The husband, according to the letter, was 70 years old - hardly an appropriate age to be swinging a pickaxe, especially when the only objective was to dig the garden.

Do make sure the goods you buy are suitable for your purpose. If you buy over the internet, ask the prospective supplier: ' Is this product suitable for all soil types?' Don't purchase until you get a clear answer. If you communicate with the supplier by email, keep the emails on file. If the product fails to live up to expectations, then lodge a complaint, and persevere until you get satisfaction.

The gardening discussion forums on the internet are a ideal place to post messages about such problems, but make sure that you don't fall foul of the laws of defamation. If you do have a problem with a supplier, tell them that you will be posting their replies on gardening forums, or that you are considering doing so (see chapter 2). This should spur them into action. Most companies will move mountains to avoid bad PR.

Ergonomics, disabilities and ageing

Many older people eventually have to give up gardening, because they can no longer cope with its physical demands. Yet ergonomics is developing new kinds of tools that can help people remain active for longer.

Adao Tools
http://www.adao.com/products/mainpr16.html
A range of long-handled tools can be found at Adao Tools. This Californian company offers a number of well-designed long-handled products.

Age Net
http://www.agenet.com/ergo.garden.tools.html
Age Net makes a product called the ergonomic garden tool set (figure 38). The set contains a hoe, spade and cultivator and is fabricated of plastic and stainless steel. This is suitable of those of limited hand strength and they say it can be held in a comfortable, neutral position.

Fig. 38. Agenet offers some helpful information about a range of products to help with gardening.

Gardening health and safety..

Fig. 39. The web site of Frostproof, which supplies specialist gardening tools such as this ratchet pruner.

FrostProof.com
http://www.frostproof.com/catalog/hb-570.html
Carpal Tunnel Syndrome affects the carpals, a set of bones in the hand. The result is that the sufferer experiences great difficulty in gripping, with a severe impact on their ability to garden. Frost Proof (figure 39) offers solutions over the internet with its ergonomically designed tools. They say they regularly ship deliveries to Europe without experiencing problems. They can supply UK customers.

Gardenscape
http://www.gardenscape.on.ca/pages/enablingtools.htm
Check out this Canadian site and its 'enabling tools' page. It also sells Peta tools mentioned below and a wide range of other interesting products. We particularly liked the EZ Reacher ('easy reacher'). This is ideal both in the garden and at home, if you have difficulty in bending to pick up dropped things. We also liked the look of their ergonomically designed pruners. All prices are listed in Canadian dollars, so you will need to work out the exchange rate and be ready to pay something for shipping. Their enabling tools mean that there is probably something there that helps a disabled person to garden.

Indiana Hand Center
http://www.indianahandcenter.com/easgardn.html
We were impressed by the quality of advice available on the internet,

Fig. 40. The Indiana Handcenter is a mine of information about the human hand and how to protect it while working.

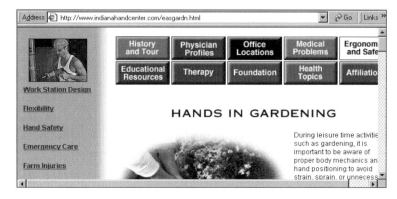

regarding hands in the garden. Good advice can be had from an organisation called the Indiana Hand Centre (figure 40) whose web site is worth bookmarking/adding to favourites. It contains excellent advice, in particular for the older gardener.

The Left Hand
http://www.thelefthand.com
Being left-handed is not a disability, but if you are left-handed you will know the practical problems associated with living in a right-handed world. This site is worth a visit (figure 41). It has a number of gardening tools designed for left-handed people. Once again it is a US site and a US company. We would have liked to recommend similar British or European companies, but could find none listed on the search engines.

Fig. 41. Left Hand claims to be the largest retailer of products for left-handed people. The links on the left show some of its product categories (scroll down for more).

Peta
http://www.peta-uk.com/
Based in Essex, Peta designs gardening tools for physically disabled people. Its motto is 'innovating for independence'. If you have someone in the family who is less agile than once they were, this site is well worth visiting (figure 42). It describes how the tools have been adapted and shows diagrams of the various products. Peta also has a range of products called Scissorcraft, useful if you have trouble with conventional scissors. Peta works closely with occupational therapists and organisa-

Fig. 42. Peta UK, supplier of Scissorcraft products and ergonomically designed garden hand tools.

tions such as Disabled Living Foundation and Disability Trust, to try and meet the needs of disabled gardeners. Peta has also been involved in 'horticultural therapy', designed to help people with mental or physical illness.

Rakehandle
http://www.rakehandle.com
We have already mentioned long handles and the wisdom of avoiding back strain. One interesting device from the USA is the 'Upper Hand universal handle' (figure 43). This is an ergonomic handle for rakes, shovels, and lawn garden use. The Upper Hand auxiliary handle is back-saving and helps reduce strain on the lower back. It clips onto the shaft of a long handled tool. It also reduces blisters and is well worth looking at, even if you are not disabled.

Fig. 43. Rakehandle, an ergonomically designed product from a company of the same name.

Stanley Tools
http://www.stanleyworks.com
American firms continue to dominate ecommerce, but this is the web site of the famous UK firm of Stanley Tools, and one that is well worth book-marking. The firm takes a scientific approach to product development, and has called in university specialists to research how tools can be developed to make physical work easier. Their site lists a number of their products which they describe as ergonomic. It should be noted there is no industry standard defining the term ergonomic.

Total Living Company
http://www.totalliving.com
If your needs are more general than just the garden, take a look at the Total Living Company. It offers a substantial number of goodies that are ergonomically designed and can help you in all aspects of your life.

Tiger Tooth Folding Saws
http://www.barnel.com/folding.html
Saws, too, are available in ergonomic designs and we were pleased to find them available online. Tiger Tooth is certainly worth a visit (figure 44).

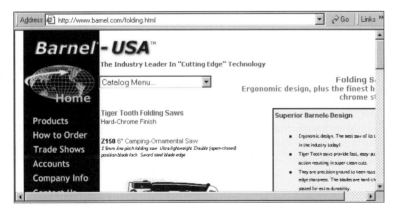

Fig. 44. Tiger Tooth folding saws.

Using electrical tools

Wagner Spraytech
http://www.wagnerspraytech.co.uk/cordless.htm
Another problem for the disabled or older gardener is dealing safely and effectively with electrical equipment. For instance, strimmers are a pain when you have to deal with them from a seated position. The cables drag across the garden, which can be especially dangerous if there are water features, or even puddles of rain water. Clearly, electrical machines pose problems. One possible answer is UK-based Wagner Spraytech which supplies strimmers fitted with rechargeable batteries (figure 45).

Fig. 45. Wagner Spray-tech, suppliers of cordless string strimmers.

When it comes to dealing with electrical equipment, and machines like ride-on mowers and tractors used in large gardens, clear thinking about ergonomics is vital. Without it accidents can and do happen. If you are going to buy heavy electrical equipment, consider several aspects of ergonomic design before making your purchase.

Consider your main physical needs:

1. Does the product provide you with the required level of comfort?
2. If there is an engine, are the emission levels acceptable?
3. Will you need to use the equipment on a regular basis or only occasionally?
4. Where will you store the equipment?

Gardening health and safety..

Items of machinery like ride-on tractors are heavy, and nothing is more apt to produce accidents than the inappropriate use of heavy machinery in a domestic setting. This can mean more than just backache that cures itself in a few days, but serious spinal injury and even nerve damage.

Power-to-weight ratios

To reduce the risks, look for a high power-to-weight ratio. This is more difficult than it might seem. A piece of equipment that is physically light enough to handle may lack the power to do the jobs that you want. Look at the centre of gravity of any ride-on vehicle, especially if you have a garden with hills or rises. Ride-on equipment with a low centre of gravity is harder to topple over.

If you really do need a particular machine, and it has a high centre of gravity, then consider getting a roll bar fitted. This is a solid, strong bar that rises above the height of the driver when s/he is in the seat. Should an accident take place as you are coming down a hill, then, as the machine rolls over, the roll bar takes the weight and keeps it from crushing the driver. We have relatives who are now retired farmers and through them know of a number of farmers who were killed in similar accidents on farms.

Vibration

Consider the vibration level of the machine. We bought an excellent strimmer, but forty minutes after using it, Graham complains that his fingers are still tingling from the vibration.

Many ergonomically designed machines possess anti-vibration systems. These separate the engine from the handle of the machine. Don't forget ear and eye protection as well. Ear-guards are essential, as are goggles. If you wear glasses, we recommend wearing goggles on top of the glasses. Things can fly about: glasses will not protect the side of your eyes, but goggles will. We recently read of a case where the user of a strimmer was in substantial pain, after not wearing eye protection, since he had something lodged behind his eyeball. It can happen.

Similarly, if you are doing work like logging, make sure you have helmet protection.

If you intend using noisy machines like chainsaws, you can buy helmets with eye and ear protection built in. This is good ergonomics, and good economics too. If you become ill because of poor equipment, this could really hit you financially. It is better to avoid this if at all possible. If you do not get the level of comfort you require, do not buy the product. Don't let yourself be short-changed. If you cannot get the product you want in the UK, by using the internet you will probably be able to get it elsewhere.

Raised beds for easier gardening

One thing to consider is using the raised bed system. This means raising beds to about one metre (about three feet) high. These can be made from breeze blocks or built up with wooden sides. Your garden beds will then be about the height of the display stands that you see in many garden centres. This is an ideal height for a wheelchair-bound gardener. The big downside is the sheer volume of soil needed to build the raised beds. Yet this could – relatively - be a small price to pay for extended gardening time in later years.

One tip is to fill a proportion of the beds with well-rotted horse-manure. This needs to be mixed with some good quality topsoil. It will provide abundant nutrients for your plants. However, if you do fill the beds with horse manure, you really need to leave them for about a year. This is because of the microbiological action that takes place within the manure itself. Horse manure heats up considerably, and can literally scorch the roots of young plants. We have seen the inside of hot beds which have heated up in this way. They can become so hot that ash forms where the heat has burned the straw in the manure. However, when it is about a year old, and well mixed with topsoil, it provides great nourishment for plants.

Gardening as therapy

Linda
http://www.geocities.com/Heartland/Pointe/8391/recovery.html
If you want an example of the power of therapy, and how horticulture can help, visit Linda's web site at the 'virtual community' of Geocities (figure 46). It tells the inspiring story of how a young woman, aged 36, was diagnosed with breast cancer. She relates how she battled and won her fight, with the help of her garden.

Fig. 46. Linda's recovery garden. Her web site contains an inspirational account of gardening as therapy after undergoing major surgery,

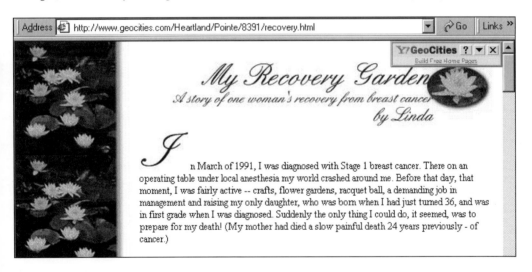

Address http://www.geocities.com/Heartland/Pointe/8391/recovery.html ▾ ⟳ Go ‖ Links »

Y/GeoCities ? ▾ X
Build Free Home Pages

My Recovery Garden
A story of one woman's recovery from breast cancer
by Linda

n March of 1991, I was diagnosed with Stage 1 breast cancer. There on an operating table under local anesthesia my world crashed around me. Before that day, that moment, I was fairly active -- crafts, flower gardens, racquet ball, a demanding job in management and raising my only daughter, who was born when I had just turned 36, and was in first grade when I was diagnosed. Suddenly the only thing I could do, it seemed, was to prepare for my death! (My mother had died a slow painful death 24 years previously - of cancer.)

5 Organic gardening

In this chapter we will explore:

▶ *how to get started*
▶ *taking care of the soil*
▶ *where do you get worm compost?*
▶ *how to feed your soil*
▶ *pest control the organic way*
▶ *weed control without chemicals*
▶ *dealing with disease*

Gardening organically means that you garden without the use of inorganic chemicals such as pesticides, herbicides and fertilisers. But it is also the philosophy of working in harmony with nature rather than against it. It means looking after the soil and keeping it in good heart so that it will keep on producing healthy plants year after year, without having to continually dump chemicals onto it and onto your plants. Organic gardening is about striking a balance between you, your plot, and nature, and taking advantage of what nature can do for you. It is also about caring for the environment as a whole and not doing anything that may damage the environment.

By adopting an holistic approach you will get this balance right and nature will eventually take care of most of your pest and disease problems for you with very little help from you. And it will reward you with healthy flowers, fruit and vegetables. You will have the satisfaction of knowing that what went into growing them is not going to damage you or your family's health or the environment.

Henry Doubleday Research Association
http://www.hdra.org.uk
The HDRA is dedicated to promoting organic gardening. At the time of writing, they are running a Grow Your Own campaign aimed at encouraging people to grow their own food, or some of it. You will find lots of useful information here and can search the site for leaflets on just about anything to do with organic gardening (figure 47). If you decide to seriously adopt the organic way, you might like to join this non-profit making organisation. At the very least a visit to one or both of their gardens would be worthwhile and make an interesting and informative day out.

Growing organically is not a soft option, especially if you are changing from a chemical-based growing system. In the first season, and probably for a couple of seasons afterwards it will be hard work and you need to be prepared for losses, failures and disappointments until you get the natural balance right. It may also mean you have to give up growing some things because they are just too difficult to grow well without the use of chemicals. All this means is, that a particular plant is not suited to your situation, for some reason. It could be your soil is not right, or the

Fig, 47. HDRA, an excellent site for advice on organic gardening.

microclimate is wrong, for that particular plant. Don't worry about it – move the plant to a different spot, or grow something else. There's plenty of choice, so don't be afraid to experiment.

How to get started

The first decision you have to make is not to use inorganic chemicals in your garden any more. It's easy enough to say but not quite so easy to do, because you can't simply replace them with organic equivalents and continue as before. In fact, it may be that you have to continue using chemicals in some parts of your garden. Lawns are a case in point, especially if you have a large area of grass to look after. This is because there is no effective organic weed killer for use on lawns. In the organic world of gardening, weeds are destroyed by using a hoe, pulling them out by hand, or by covering them up and not allowing light to get to them. Obviously none of these options is practical except on the smallest of lawns.

So what do you do? You could get rid of the grass altogether and put down gravel and paving, or decking, or make some new beds. If that's not an option then growing a wild flower lawn is another idea. If the thought of long grass until late July puts you off then learning to live with a few weeds in your lawn might be a better idea. And if you are going to switch to organic gardening completely and you still want a lawn, then you have very little choice. But there are a few things you can do to make life a little easier and you lawn at least presentable.

Feeding your grass in spring by scattering it with very fine worm compost, or sieved soil mixed with a general organic fertiliser such as blood, fish and bone, will encourage the grass roots to grow and help crowd out weeds. Do this before rain is expected and the soil is moist or you will need to water it in. During the summer lift the blades of your mower and cut the grass little and often. This encourages the grass to thicken up and helps get rid of weeds that dislike being constantly cut down. Dig out daisies and other perennial weeds as they appear and never let them seed. Replace them with fine soil mixed with new grass seed. Keep moist until the new seeds are well established. In autumn rake the grass with a lawn rake to remove dead grass, moss and surface rooting weeds. Aerate the lawn surface with a fork, pushing the tines into the grass every six inches. Brush a mixture of silver or course sand and sieved compost over the surface. This allows air into the soil and improves drainage.

Alan Titchmarsh and Organic Gardening
http://www.bbc.co.uk/homeandgarden/gardening/
Alternatively, you can do what Alan Titchmarsh does at Barleywood, and compromise. He gardens organically except for his lawn where he uses a chemical lawn weed and feed preparation in spring to get rid of the weeds. And if we had a lawn the size of his we may do as well. You can find out all about Barleywood and Alan Titchmarsh at the BBC Gardener's World web site.

Organic Gardening Magazine
http://www.organicgardening.com
A good starting point is to visit the web site of the American magazine *Organic Gardening* (figure 48). It has a useful feature called Steps to Organic Gardening that will help you make a start. There are also some interesting articles available for you to read that will give you a taster of what organic gardening is all about.

Suite 101
http://suite101.com
Another site that has some useful information for organic gardening

Fig. 48. Organic Gardening Magazine is packed with useful features and contacts.

Fig. 49. Suite 101 offers some useful information about organic gardening for beginners.

beginners is Suite 101 (figure 49). Look for the 'home & garden button' then go to 'beginning organic gardening'. This site has pages and pages of interesting information for gardeners so you might want to add it to your bookmarks.

Once you've made the decision to turn organic, it's a good idea to get rid of any garden chemicals lurking in your shed, garage or greenhouse. That way you won't be tempted to turn to them at the first sign of blackfly on your roses in spring. Don't put them in the dustbin or pour them down the sink. Dispose of them safely by contacting your local authority's environment department and ask them what you should do with them. If your authority has a web site then you can probably get the information from there. Most authorities have some central collection point where you can take unwanted garden chemicals for safe disposal.

Taking care of the soil

The most important part of gardening organically is to look after your soil. A healthy, productive soil will produce healthy, strong plants that are better able to withstand pest and disease attacks. And as the plants we grow take a lot out of our garden soils by way of nutrients, we have to be continually replacing these elements.

Nature manages to replace the nutrients taken up by plants growing in the wild by breaking down dead organic matter, such as leaves, and turning it into new soil. Micro-organisms and other soil inhabitants such as worms perform this task very well in nature. But because we cultivate our plants much more intensely than nature does, we have to give nature a helping hand.

There are several ways to do this. The first is to improve the structure of your soil by adding plenty of organic matter. The ideal soil structure allows excess water to drain away but also retains moisture. This may seem a contradiction, but what it means is that regardless of the type of soil, sandy, clay, chalky, loam, stony etc. it will not become waterlogged when it rains, nor will it dry out at the first hint of sunshine. Good soil structure also allows air to penetrate without which plants will die.

Well-rotted manure, garden compost, leaf mould, and spent mushroom compost are ideal for improving soil structure. You can obtain these and other different sorts of soil conditioner from garden centres and nurseries, or you can make your own compost. It's not difficult if you follow the rules. There are plenty of places to go for help and advice with making compost whether you make it in a bought in bin or construct your own.

Henry Doubleday Research Association
http://hdra.org.uk
We have already mentioned HDRA. It has a useful guide to making compost.

RotWeb
http://net.indra.co/-topsoil/compost
Another interesting site to visit for information on compost making is

RotWeb. This somewhat quirky site is dedicated to compost and com-posting. You should be able to pick up some useful tips and information from here.

Virtual Garden

http://www.vg.com

The Virtual Garden, too, has lots of information on compost making (figure 50).

Fig. 50. The Virtual Garden has lots of information on successful compost making.

Waste Watch

http://www.wastewatch.org.uk/links/linksmain.htm

Throughout the developed world we still fail to recycle enough of our waste. This site is packed with information including links on compost.

We have not so far mentioned using peat. This is not only because peat lacks nutrients, but the digging of peat from ancient peat bogs in Ireland and UK is damaging to the environment. Commercial peat-digging for horticultural purposes endangers what remains of our wetland habitats, which are rare and support rare wildlife. Once the peat is dug up the wetland habitats and their wildlife will disappear forever, and cannot be replaced.

In any case, peat is unnecessary in our gardens. Gardeners managed pretty well before its introduction in the late 1950s with the use of loam-based products. Today there are plenty of good substitutes on the market such as composted bark products, composted straw and composted coir. All of these make good soil conditioners and are already being used as a peat substitute in potting and sowing composts. As we are writing this, we have heard that the National Trust has banned the use of peat at all of its properties, of which 50% were peat-free zones before this announcement. This is good news and will encourage many gardeners to follow suite.

Royal Society for the Protection of Birds
http://www.rspb.org
For information on the issue of peat, and for details of suppliers of peat free composts, take a look at the RSPB web site.

What else can be used to improve soil condition? Worm compost is perhaps the best conditioner of all because it improves soil structure and feeds it at the same time with a lot of nutrients. It can be used on its own and dug into the top 5cm (2ins) of soil if your soil needs a lot of feeding, or mixed with garden compost to make it go further.

Where do you get worm compost?

There are a few suppliers around the country and you may be lucky enough to find one near you. Otherwise you can get it by mail order, or make it yourself.

Wiggly Wigglers
http://www.wigglywigglers.co.uk
One web site to visit to find out all about worms, worm compost, and how to make it, is Wiggly Wigglers (figure 51). It provides everything for making worm compost at home, and has lots of information about worms and what they do, and a useful selection of books as well.

Fig. 51. Wiggley Wigglers, a site which tells you all about worms, and how to produce good quality worm compost.

Fig. 52. The web site of the Worm Woman, Mary Applehof, a fount of knowledge about 'vermicomposting'.

Worm Woman
http://www.wormwoman.com
Another good site for finding out about the value of worm compost is Worm Woman (figure 52). Mary Applehof is the real Worm Woman, famous for her best selling book *Worms Eat My Garbage*. She and two assistants run Flower Fields Publishing, a company dedicated to spreading the word about the benefits of worms and worm compost.

Feeding your soil

Having improved the structure and condition of your soil, you may also need to feed it, particularly if your soil is sandy and tends to drain very quickly. Nutrients are quickly lost from fast draining soils by leaching.

How do you know if your soil needs feeding?
If it's producing healthy plants, plenty of flowers and good yields of vegetables and fruit then it probably doesn't need any extra food. However, if plants are small and yields are poor you may need to give your soil a helping hand by adding some extra fertiliser.

This can be done by incorporating more garden compost, well rotted manure or worm compost into the top 5cm (2ins) of soil, or by using some other organic fertiliser. The best kind of fertiliser to use for general application is a balanced one, that provides nitrogen, phosphate and potash. Blood, fish and bone is a good, well balanced, general purpose, organic fertiliser. Another is dried and pelleted poultry manure, which many gardeners prefer. Seaweed meal is also extremely good, if a little expensive. Other things to consider are dried sewage sludge, spent mushroom compost, and spent hops from a brewery. Getting hold of these may depend on where you live and what is available locally.

These fertilisers should be applied in spring shortly before planting and raked into the soil surface. They can also be applied during the season after removing one crop and just before planting the next crop. They can also be used as an early spring dressing for over wintering crops such as onions. Follow the instructions on the packet carefully and do not over use. Too much nitrogen can cause plants to put on excessive leaf growth at the expense of flowers. Excessive leaf growth also makes plants vulnerable to attack from pests and diseases.

Another way to feed and condition the soil at the same time, is to grow green manure. You do this by sowing seeds of the green manure plant, for example grazing rye, on a vacant piece of ground, allowing it to grow and then digging it in before it flowers. Grazing rye is sown in late summer or autumn and dug in during the spring. There are several types of green manure available for sowing at different times of year and on different types of soil. In addition to feeding and conditioning soil, green manure protects bare soil from weather damage, and from being colonised by weeds.

The magic of comfrey
Although this is not strictly speaking a green manure, comfrey is widely grown by organic gardeners as a cheap source of nutrients for plants. Comfrey grows so fast that they do not have time to become woody.

This means that the nitrogen, potash and phosphorous stored in its leaves and stems becomes instantly available for other plants to use. And because its roots go down from 1.3 to 2.6m it collects food that would otherwise be unavailable.

Comfrey can be cut 4 or 5 times a season to provide a mulch for plants that need extra potassium such as tomatoes and potatoes. An established bed of 12 comfrey plants will produce 2 cwt of cut comfrey in a season. A bed planted in September from cuttings will be ready in June for the first cut. A comfrey bed, if well maintained, should have a productive life of at least 20 years.

Comfrey can also be made into a liquid by fermenting the cut leaves in a covered barrel of water for several weeks. The liquid is then drained off and bottled. It is used as a liquid feed for plants such as tomatoes. An alternative method is to make the liquid without water again allowing the cut leaves to ferment and drawing off the black liquid. This is then diluted with water at about 20 parts water to 1 of comfrey liquid and used in the same way. Bocking 14 is the strain of comfrey normally recommended for garden use.

Paul's Garden World
http://www.powen.freeserve.co.uk/Projects/Comfrey.htm
This is a superb site, which tells you how to construct a comfrey press. A comfrey press is a contraption that helps you crush comfrey plants and thereby make plant food. There is also an excellent link to fertilizers.

Other methods of creating a productive soil
One of the main ways of keeping soil healthy and productive in the vegetable garden is to practise crop rotation. This means not growing the same crop in the same place year after year. There are some exceptions to this rule. Asparagus is one, and comfrey another.

Crops like potatoes, beans and peas, onions and leeks, brassicas and other members of the cabbage family, and root crops such as carrots, parsnips and turnips, should be moved around the plot from year to year. This avoids pests and diseases becoming established in any one area. Other crops such as salads can be grown wherever there is space for them. Crop rotation becomes relatively easy if the vegetable plot or allotment is divided into beds rather than being treated as a whole in the traditional way.

Henry Doubleday Research Association
http://hdra.org.uk
HDRA has some good information on crop rotation and green manure on its web site. It has a useful chart of plant families and an example of a basic four-year rotation.

Pest control the organic way

Once you get the natural balance right in your garden, pest control with sprays will be a thing of the past. The secret of controlling garden pests is to attract their predators onto your plot. This means making your garden wildlife-friendly. Birds are the most obvious form of wildlife to attract as they eat an enormous amount of insects, especially during the breeding season. Blue tits, in particular, are very fond of aphids such as green and white fly. They also like caterpillars. Robins and blackbirds will regularly sweep your garden for juicy morsels.

To get them to visit your garden you must make it attractive for them. This means putting out food and water for them all year round, not just in winter. This way they will recognise your garden as a place to come for food and will visit it regularly, perhaps several times a day. A simple bird table is better then just throwing the food on the ground, because birds such as blue tits and green finches prefer to feed this way. Put food on the ground as well to attract blackbirds, thrushes and sparrows, which are ground feeders.

Royal Society for the Protection of Birds
http://www.rspb.org.uk
Another way of attracting birds is to grow shrubs and small trees that will provide perching areas, cover and nesting sites. Flowering plants also attract insects, which in turn attract birds. Try to make your garden a cat-free zone and never put a bird table or nesting box near a fence where cats can reach it. For further details on how to attract birds to your garden, and all about bird tables, visit the RSPB web site.

In addition to birds other types of wildlife can be attracted into the garden to get rid of pests. These include frogs and toads, beetles such as stag beetles, ladybirds and lacewings, hedgehogs and bats. Much of this wildlife will be attracted if you provide a pond specifically for wildlife. You can find out how to make a wildlife pond at the RSPB web site mentioned above. It will attract frogs, toads, insects, birds and small mammals such as hedgehogs.

Other measures you can take are to provide dark places for animals to hide. This might be a small pile of stones or bricks in a quiet corner of your garden where beetles can congregate. A pile of old logs built to make a miniature den is the ideal over-wintering spot for hedgehogs, as is beneath a shed. Frogs will hide in damp places underneath groundcover plants, especially if they are close to or overhanging water. Lacewings can be provided with a lacewing hotel made from a loosely rolled piece of corrugated cardboard hung up in a tree.

Bat Conservation Trust
http://www.bats.org.uk
Bats will visit your garden if you put up nesting boxes for them. For information on bats, how to attract them to your garden and on making bat boxes go to the Bat Conservation Trust site (figure 53).

Another method of overcoming pests is to prevent them from reaching your plants. This is particularly useful when growing vegetables. For example, carrot fly can be controlled, by growing carrots under fleece. The fleece is put in place as soon as the seedlings appear and remains there until the crop has finished. The disadvantage with this method is that it attracts slugs, which love the damp conditions under the fleece.

Fig. 53. The home page of the Bat Conservation Trust.

An alternative is to surround the carrots with a fence of fleece a couple of feet high but leave them uncovered. This prevents the female carrot fly, which flies at ground level, reaching the carrots, and does not attract slugs. Similarly, cabbages and other brassicas can be protected from cabbage root fly by surrounding the stems at ground level with a collar. Buy these at a garden centre or make your own from thick cardboard, newspaper or plastic.

To protect the cabbage family from caterpillars in late summer, net the crops with a fine mesh netting before the butterflies appear. We net our cabbage family plants as soon as they are planted and keep them netted until the crop is cleared from the ground. This keeps off the cabbage white butterflies and birds such as pigeons that would strip the leaves to a skeleton if they could.

Netting can also be used to keep birds off newly planted seeds. And fleece can be used to protect autumn sown beans and peas from mice. It also protects these crops from frost damage and very heavy rain.

Another well-known method for dealing with insect pest used by organic gardeners is companion planting. The theory is that certain plants repel certain insects so if that plant is grown next to a crop that has a particular insect problem the insects will be repelled. For example, marigolds are known to repel whitefly. This is because they contain a natural insecticide toxic to whitefly. They are, therefore, often planted amongst greenhouse tomato crops, which suffer badly from aphids. This seems to work quite well and the best type of marigold to use is the Tagetes. Another commonly mentioned companionship is to grow onions amongst carrots. It is said the smell of the onions confuses the carrot fly and protects the carrots from infestation. We have our doubts about this. You may like to try it and see if it works.

The introduction of individual predator species is becoming quite common in the fight against insect pests, particularly in greenhouses. In the commercial world the use of predators, such as the encarsia wasp against aphid attack in greenhouses, is wide spread. These treatments are available to the amateur and, although relatively expensive, are growing in popularity. So far they are only suitable for use in glass houses, and need to be introduced at the correct time to have any effect, before the pest has built up a large population.

If all else fails then there are organic sprays available at garden centres, but these have limited effect on large populations. It might be better to wait for the predator to arrive, as it surely will. In the meantime, remove the pests by hand to keep down the population and prevent the problem getting out of control. Vigilance and frequent observation of what is happening in your garden will pay big dividend.

The Dirt Doctor
http://www.dirtdoctor.com
One web site to visit which has a number of home-made remedies for insect pests is The Dirt Doctor (figure 54). This American site is written by a Texan organic gardening writer and broadcaster, so the tips are mainly relevant only to this part of the world, e.g. his advice about dealing with invading armadillos.

Fig. 54. The Dirt Doctor (Howard Garrett) is an online source of home-made remedies for dealing with insect pest.

Slugs and snails
One of the worst pests that organic gardeners complain about is slugs. Non-organic gardeners complain bitterly about them, too. As our winters become wetter and warmer, slugs (and snails) seem to be active all year round.

With no slug pellets to poison them with, the organic gardener has to look for other solutions. One often recommended remedy is a trap called the slug pub. This is a container filled with beer (or milk) that is pushed into the ground. Slugs are attracted to the beer and fall in and drown. In theory this seems a good idea. Unfortunately, the slug pub attracts friendly animals such as ground beetles, which also fall in and drown.

Another way of trapping slugs is to sink upturned grapefruit halves into the soil and collect the slugs that hide under them every morning. Putting down some tasty food for them and collecting them up after dark when they come out to feed is another idea. Many organic gardeners go out with a torch every night and collect up every one they come across. Whilst these ideas may help to keep down the population, other techniques need to be employed to protect vulnerable plants.

Most seedlings and young plants are vulnerable to slug and snail attack. These pests love the young tender leaves and it is not uncommon to have a whole row of emerging seedlings disappear overnight. It's happened to us on more than one occasion, and they don't seem to be particularly fussy about what they eat. One way of protecting young plants is to stop the slugs getting to them by putting a barrier around them. Grit, crushed eggshells, sharp sand, soot, even a sprinkling of salt are all worth trying. Plastic collars made from drinks bottles are also useful for individual plants such as hostas. Sink the collar at least 1 cm into the ground. Unfortunately, slugs and snails are excellent climbers so this idea may only be partially effective. However, it may give protection long enough for the plants to become established.

None of these techniques will rid your garden of slugs and snails completely. But if you are vigilant in collecting those you find, and also attract their predators, particularly beetles, frogs, birds and hedgehogs, into your garden, you can be certain that a balance will eventually be reached and populations will not get out of hand.

Weed control without chemicals

As previously mentioned, to control weeds without using chemicals, organic gardeners use a sharp hoe and employ the technique of mulching. A sharp hoe will cut weeds off at ground level where they can be left to wither and die or collected and put on the compost heap. Hoeing also disturbs surface weed seeds, making it less easy for them to get established. If you hoe regularly and follow the golden rule of never letting weeds seed themselves, your patch should be virtually free from annual within two to three seasons.

Perennial weeds are a little more difficult to eradicate. These need to be got rid of when the ground is being prepared for planting. Dig the soil over thoroughly and remove all signs of perennial weeds such as couch grass, horsetail, bindweed, thistles, dandelions, brambles, nettles, docks, buttercup, ground elder, grass weeds etc., including all roots. Whenever a perennial weed starts growing, pull it up immediately roots and all. Leave it to dry and then put on the compost heap. Eventually, most perennial weeds will disappear but it could take a few seasons.

Removing weeds also helps eradicate pests because it destroys many plants that play host to unwelcome insects such as aphids. Cleanliness and hygiene in the garden are vital to successful organic gardening, both as a means of deterring pests and cutting down on the potential for disease.

The other main weapon against weeds is the technique of mulching. Mulching not only eradicates weeds by smothering them, it also prevents them from seeding because the soil is covered up. You can use garden compost, rotted manure, worm compost, shredded bark, spent mushroom compost, gravel and pebbles as a mulch. Shredded newspaper and cardboard, black plastic, porous membranes, fleece, and even old fertiliser bags can all be used to mulch the ground. The golden rule is never to leave ground uncovered. Nature will fill it with unwanted plants (weeds) if you do.

Dealing with disease

The best way of coping with disease is to avoid it where possible. Clean-

Organic gardening ....

liness and hygiene in the garden at all times is a golden rule, just as it would be in your house. This means clearing up all dead and dying organic matter such as leaves, weeds, flowers and vegetables that have finished, on a regular basis and consigning the material to the compost heap. When sowing seeds in trays or pots always use new, fresh compost from a reliable source. And wash the trays and pots thoroughly before sowing. Use a copper fungicide sprayed lightly onto the compost surface before sowing the seeds. This helps prevent damping off diseases and mildew. Greenhouse surfaces need to be thoroughly cleaned and disinfected at least once a year. And never store pots and trays without first washing them. If you apply the same cleanliness and hygiene rules to the garden as you would to your home you won't go far wrong.

Another way of avoiding disease is to choose your plants with care and grow disease resistant varieties. For example, there are many roses that are resistant to rose black spot, and many vegetables are bred to resist the more common diseases.

If you only choose healthy plants and grow them well, then they will be more able to resist disease if and when it does attack. And by continually observing what is happening to your plants you should be able to spot the first signs of disease. You will then be able to do something about it before the disease damages your plants. Most times, just removing the infected part is all you need to do. Occasionally, the disease may be more serious and you will have to use an organic spray. If the disease cannot be cured the whole plant will have to be destroyed.

6 Garden design

In this chapter we will explore:

▶ *creating a garden with people in mind*
▶ *planning garden utilities*
▶ *planning flower beds*
▶ *finalising your plan*
▶ *planting list and hard landscaping*
▶ *hold on, don't start planting yet*
▶ *types of garden*
▶ *some more garden design web sites*

. . . .

Creating a garden with people in mind

The best advice when redesigning a garden or planning a new one is to take your time. Think through what it is you want to achieve with the garden. The biggest temptation is to get the spade out and start digging straight away, but it's best to start with a pencil and a piece of paper. This preplanning stage will help you clarify what it is you want from your garden.

Treat the garden just as you would a room in the house. Design it to be practical and functional, but visually attractive too. You need to feel comfortable and at peace in the garden.

The late Geoff Hamilton's television series on *Paradise Gardens* was a classic example of how to design a garden to create some peace and tranquillity, a space into which you can escape and unwind after a hard day. So, in this pre-planning stage, start listing all the things you want from the garden.

▶ *A little piece of paradise* – Try to create a 'paradise garden' for yourself. In reality it may only be part of the whole garden, but if it is an area where you can go, and be quiet with nature, then it will have achieved its purpose; it will be your little piece of paradise.

Children and gardens
Some people believe that children and gardens do not go together. Yet children need a space to run off their energy. Some adults are unaware that children can get just as stressed as adults. Children face many pressures from school and examinations, and they too can appreciate a quiet area to sit in. For five minutes a day, you can encourage them to simply sit quietly and enjoy the peace of the garden; it will do wonders for them. When designing your garden, try and keep their needs in mind.

If your children are small, it is better not to have a garden pond. A toddler can drown in just a few inches of water, so it is better not to risk it until they are older. Instead of a pond, plan and dig a hole where you would like the pond to be, but create a sand pit. This will give young children hours of fun and be perfectly safe. Make sure that you buy 'play sand' from the merchants. This is a specially designed and safe product. Later, when the children are older, you can dig it out and that will be the site of your pond.

Gardens and older people

Consider other adult family members, too. What about elderly individuals? Even if they do not live with you, give thought to questions of access to the garden. One older couple paid out £14,000 to have their garden professionally landscaped. A wonderful job was done, but it left them with some steep steps without handrails. The husband began to lose his sight and the couple was forced to move house because the garden became too hazardous for him. So, if you have older people in the family, don't make any steps too steep, and be sure to include some solid hand-rails in your design. Similarly, make sure that any pathways are not likely to become slippery.

If there is an elderly wheelchair bound or disabled family member, you will also need to plan suitable access to the garden – both to and from the house and through the garden gate to the road outside. Anyone who has pushed a wheelchair knows how demanding this can be. So if you have to build a ramp, do not make it too steep. Ideally a ramp should be on a slight incline, with a level part at the top, where the wheelchair can be halted. The person in the chair can then negotiate the ramp him or herself and not have to depend on others. It also means that with the level part at the top, they can open doors without the chair running dangerously back on them.

As far as the garden design goes, you may need to allow space for a ramp. Again, if you are building your own ramp, make sure that you fit suitable hand-rails and that the surface is not prone to be slippery. It is also worth calculating the turning circle required by a chair. Avoid planting too close to the bottom of the ramp, to leave enough space for the chair user to turn. It is also sensible to avoid planting prickly things, like roses, too close to pathways. When plants like this grow a little too long, they can even be a nuisance to the able-bodied by catching and tearing coats and bags, but the wheelchair user could be caught in the face. With a little forethought, a design solution can be found for all such problems.

Meeting your own needs

In the rush to make sure everyone else is happy, don't ignore what you yourself want from the garden. Make a list of what it is you want to achieve. Have a look at several different gardening books, and then do the unthinkable – be ready to break some rules. Some gardeners are apt to become victims of their own strict rules.

Can we afford it?

Money is an issue with most people. When it comes to making a garden it is possible to go crazy and spend a fortune. But this should not be necessary. Some gardeners have built paths from old skip rubbish that builders are glad to get rid of, sometimes for a few pounds, sometimes for free.

On television Geoff Hamilton once created part of a path from some old roof tiles. This was rather a neat idea. Most people would have laid the tiles flat, but as soon as they were walked on, they would have shattered. But Geoff cannily laid them on end in a deeper hole. By doing it this way, he created an attractive feature for one of his gardens. Another idea is to use other gardening contacts and see what seeds or plants you can beg from them. Most fellow gardeners are generous-minded and will let you have cuttings or even sometimes full plants. You don't need spend a fortune to create a beautiful garden.

Planning garden utilities

First of all, decide on the functional elements of the garden. Where do you want the bin to be housed? It needs to be close enough to the kitchen door, to enable people to empty the internal bins, but far enough away so that any smells do not cause nuisance. It also needs to be not too far from the gate, so that whoever takes it out for the refuse collectors is not left with a mountain of a job in having to shift it. Bad backs are no joke. The modern wheelie bin is a great development, especially for the older person.

Drying area

Where do you plan to locate your drying area? One of the worst aspects of many garden designs are ugly clothes lines crossing the garden like spaghetti. When designing a new garden, you can have a rotating clothes dryer that can be placed into a stand, used, and then put away in the garden shed until the next time. Or buy a retractable clothes line that can be pulled out from the side of the house, and retracted when not in use. Again, think about the type of standing you need under the drying area. Many gardeners simply stick their drying area into the lawn. That's fine until you get into autumn or winter when puddles can appear. A solid attractive base can be constructed quite cheaply from flagstones and gravel.

The garden shed

Give careful thought to this. Where in the garden can you put a shed, maybe behind a screen, so that it is functional but not obtrusive?

Building a conservatory

This may upset the purists but this is an area where you need to consider breaking the rules. Many people put the conservatory at the back of the house, regardless of which direction the house is facing. People sometime pay out thousands of pounds to erect a conservatory on a south-facing garden, only to find that it becomes far too hot to sit in, and they have to go indoors. It is better, in these circumstances, to actually build a conservatory facing south-west. This means that you will get the late evening sun as well. So if you have a house where the rear is not south-west, consider building the conservatory elsewhere in the garden. It doesn't necessarily have to be built on to the house.

If you are building a conservatory in an area where you get winter snow, try and avoid making the roof of the conservatory out of glass. Use something stronger such as corrugated plastic. The reason is that snow, lying on the roof of the house, or whatever building the conservatory is against, will melt and slide. If this snow has hardened to ice, it can come crashing down onto the roof of the conservatory, with possibly disastrous consequences. An alternative, if you have moved into a house with a glass-roofed conservatory, is to build a small retainer fence and have it pinned to the fascia of the rear of the house. This will usually be above the guttering. Then if there is any slippage, the retaining fence (it looks like a small hurdle) should slow down the slip and simply let it melt in small pieces.

A final thought when planning a conservatory is the access to windows above. We lived in a house where we had a conservatory on the rear, which had been added to the house before we moved in. The problem was that no thought had been given to decorating the outside of the upstairs windows. There are various ways around this situation. One way is to fit opening windows in the roof of the conservatory, through which you can pass a ladder. An alternative but more expensive option is to have windows fitted, either in the French style which open inwards or the newer UK-style windows which concertina, so that you can clean the outside of the window from inside.

Planning flower beds

One final thought on planning: think carefully where you will position your flower beds. This is especially important if you intend to plant up against the house. Make sure you do not breach the damp course, a thin membrane, usually about two bricks high from the ground, which stops the damp rising through your house. If you load up the soil above this level, you will encourage damp to spread through your brickwork.

Fig. 55. The Clare's Garden web site can set you thinking about your own garden plans and ideas.

Clare's Garden
http://www.derby.org/clare/garden
This delightful site has been put together by Clare Lusher (figure 55). She has discussed some basic ideas of garden design, indicating three main

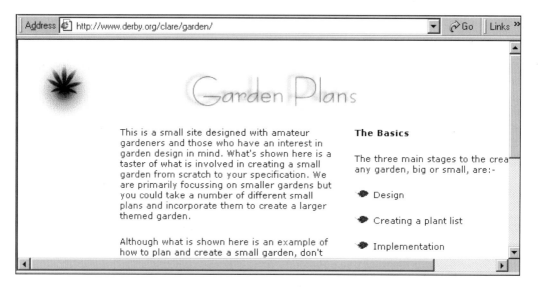

stages: design, creating a plant list, and implementation. This page links to others that talk you through other stages.

Virtual Garden
http://www.vg.com/cgi
At the time of writing, we also found some excellent advice on the American magazine web site Virtual Garden. It is a good place to find the inspiration and help you'll need to develop your projects. You can search the *Time-Life Plant Encyclopaedia*, interact with other cyber-gardeners, gather helpful hints, and explore the world of gardening online. Virtual Garden is one of the oldest gardening sites on the web.

Finalising your plan

By now you should have established exactly what it is you want from the garden. You also need to prepare a budget and to stick closely to it. There is a common myth that gardening is cheap. It can be, but it can also run away with your purse or wallet unless you are careful.

Remember, it is your garden, so you can develop it in stages. When we moved into our Somerset home, we spent three years designing and developing the garden until it came to maturity. Now we are still developing it and making changes here and there. That is the fun of gardening – and don't forget that it is supposed to be fun!

When making a plan, you are not indulging in rocket science. You are perfectly free to use an eraser, rub it out and start again. A good place to start is by drawing a map of your garden. There is a technique called triangulation. (If your garden is totally square or rectangular and your house sits square on the plot, skip this next bit). You need to measure your boundary lengths and, using a set square, draw them onto paper (see figure 56).

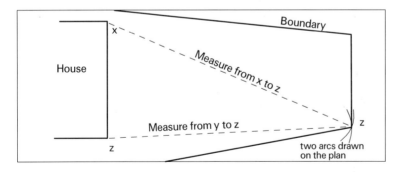

Fig. 56. A diagram to illustrate triangulation. When planning your garden, it is important to get the dimensions and measurements accurate.

However, if you are like the rest of us, you'll need to take some time and draw a plan. Builders do not always make garden plots with corners which meet at right angles. Start by measuring your house and drawing it onto a master plan. The corners of your house should be pretty close to being right angles, so you can usually trust these angles. Take a corner of your house and measure to the nearest corner of the garden. Use a clipboard to support your note-taking and draw a plan on the paper on the board. Mark your measurement onto this plan. At this stage it doesn't matter that it is rough, because we will then need to transfer it to a master plan. Repeat the process from the other corner of the house to the *same* corner of the garden. You then simply repeat the process for the other corners of the garden.

When you have done this, transfer all the measurements onto a master plan. You will need to use a pair of compasses to locate the corners of the garden in relation to the house. Use the compasses to draw arcs on the plan and this will locate the exact corners of the plot in relation to the house. Use a straightforward scale – metric is easiest, with 1 cm on paper standing for 1 metre in real life. If you would rather work in imperial, then try something like a tenth of an inch to 1 foot, which is pretty straight-forward but no where near as easy as metric.

Once you have completed the drawing of the boundaries, measure the permanent features and show them on the plan. These are things like manhole covers, trees and so on. Again, use the triangulation method to accurately locate where they lie, in relation to the house.

Shrubs and nappies, a warning
One tip, when you are planting: avoid putting shrubs too close to man-hole covers. We once lived in a house where the roots of a shrub grew under the corners of a manhole cover and down into the sewer. Two doors down, the young couple had a small baby and were forever putting nappy liners down the lavatory pan. These then caught in the roots in the sewer and blocked the sewer. It was a mature shrub and had been planted for several years, but we were obliged to move it, to prevent the same thing happening again.

Drawing the plan
One final thought for creating your plan. When you have drawn in the boundaries, ink them in on the master plan so that they show up well. Now cover the plan with a sheet of tracing paper. As you draw your master plan you may want to change things. By drawing and rubbing out on the tracing paper, you can avoid having to redraw the whole master plan.

Planting list and hard landscaping

Now comes the really fun bit, designing beds and thinking about what plants you want to grow. Consider what types of beds you want. The raised bed system has advantages, since you can grow more and have more variety. It may depend on your personal circumstances. Remember when we talked about access to the garden and wheelchair disabled people. You need to consider this when you plan the pathways. Make sure that your pathways are wide enough.

Another thing to consider is the depth of beds. In one case a person with a bad back built raised beds made from old railway sleepers, so that he could sit down and do his weeding in comfort. It took an awful lot of soil to fill the beds, but it can be an option worth considering.

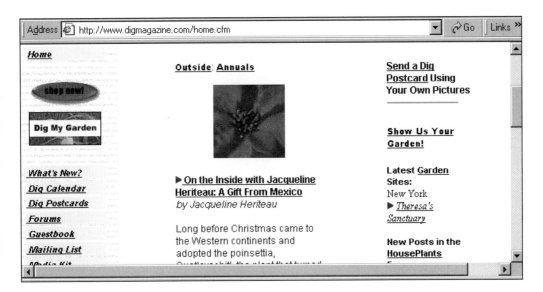

Address http://www.digmagazine.com/home.cfm

Home

shop now!

Dig My Garden

What's New?
Dig Calendar
Dig Postcards
Forums
Guestbook
Mailing List

Outside: Annuals

▶ **On the Inside with Jacqueline Heriteau: A Gift From Mexico**
by Jacqueline Heriteau

Long before Christmas came to the Western continents and adopted the poinsettia,

Send a Dig Postcard Using Your Own Pictures

Show Us Your Garden!

Latest Garden Sites:
New York
▶ *Theresa's Sanctuary*

New Posts in the HousePlants

Dig Magazine: Raised Bed Gardening
http://www.digmagazine.com/96/9-96/sylvia.cfm
Sylvia Ehrhardt has produced some useful information on raised bed gardening for the American gardening magazine, *Dig Magazine* (figure 57).

Fig. 57. The American gardening magazine, *Dig Magazine*.

Hold on, don't start planting yet

Before you start planting, get the books out and surf the net. You simply cannot stick any plant in any space and expect it to thrive. You may get lucky, but you may simply lose the plants. Decide which plants you like and which of them fit really well into the garden. Discover what each plant needs for healthy growth (see chapter three for details on gardening societies on the net). You could start by making a full list of plants that you would like and tick off those which are not suitable for one reason or another, or which would not survive.

Low-maintenance gardening
How much time have you got to work on the garden? Will the plants you have chosen require a lot of attention? The ultimate no-maintenance garden would be an area covered in concrete – but there would be no fun in that.

Check your soil
Understand the type of soil that you have in the garden. There are some simple tests that you can do for this. You also need to know whether your soil is acid or alkaline. Certain plants simply cannot thrive in the wrong type of soil. If your soil is too acidic, you may need to use lime to neutralise the acid and make it a neutral soil.

Soils Online
http://www.hintze-online.com/sos/soils-online.html
You can find more details about soils at this impressively detailed web

Garden design ....

Fig. 58. Soils Online. The site explains how you can test your own soil.

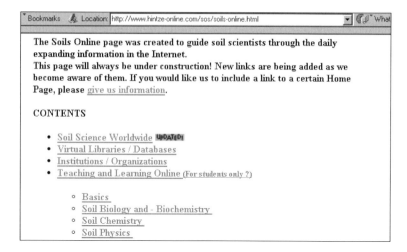

page (figure 58). You can also buy a soil-testing kit at your local garden centre. The site explains how to test your own soil.

Types of garden

There are endless types of garden one can build. It all depends on your own preferences and what you want to achieve. In this last section we will briefly discuss the different types of garden and suggest where you can find more detail on the internet.

Kitchen Gardener Online (USA)
http://www.bbg.org/gardening/kitchen/kitchen/hatch.html
Some people rather unkindly describe kitchen gardens as allotments outside the kitchen door. Yet a good kitchen garden can be as beautiful as it is functional. Take a look at Kitchen Gardener Online (figure 59). When we visited this US site (Brooklyn Botanic Garden), we found details of soil recipes, organic insecticides, a 'clay pot toad hut', a piece on double digging, fruit picking, safe gardening with manure, and a great deal more. One of its pages contained some fascinating history about Thomas Jefferson and how he created his garden.

Fig. 59. Kitchen Gardener, a web site developed by the Brooklyn Botanic Garden in New York.

More on Kitchen Gardens

http://www.bbg.org/gardening/kitchen/kitchen/simpson.html
http://www.bbg.org/gardening/kitchen/kitchen/jones.html
http://www.bbg.org/gardening/kitchen/kitchen/bales.html

Sticking with kitchen gardens, we also liked an article by John D. Simpson called: 'The four-square: a classic kitchen garden design'. There is also some fascinating detail regarding the potager, called 'A kitchen garden in the French country style' by Louisa Jones. Finally Suzy Bales has an excellent article, 'A kitchen garden in bloom: a combination cutting and vegetable garden'.

Japanese Garden Design

http://www.camera.u-net.com/gardens/japanese/basics/basics.htm

Japanese gardens may or may not be for you, but do take a look at 'The basics of Japanese garden styles'. This is a glorious and beautifully illustrated site (figure 60), containing excellent advice on how to develop a garden in this distinctive style. There is detail on hill-and-pond gardens, dry landscape gardens, tea gardens, stroll gardens, and courtyard gardens. You will also find a clickable map on the page, to show Japanese-style gardens that are open to the public in the UK and Ireland. There is also a link to the Japanese Garden Society in the UK, so if this is a favoured style of gardening for you, then you will enjoy this site.

Fig. 60. This web page is a starting point if you want to explore Japanese garden design.

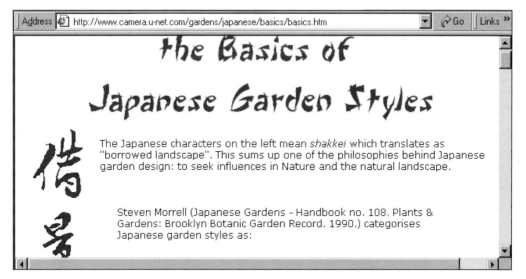

Some more garden design web sites

3D Garden Composer (USA)

http://www.gardencomposer.com

3D Garden Composer is an American software kit for garden design, planning, and landscaping. It includes a plant care calendar, an encyclopedia of plants, advice on plant diseases, 3D objects, landscape and garden plans, and various gardening tools.

Garden design ....

The Garden Wheel (USA)
http://www.gardenwheel.com
The Garden Wheel aims to make garden planning and design easy, and fun. You can select from eight garden wheels, including a perennial garden wheel, annual garden wheel, herb garden wheel, vegetable garden wheel, shade garden wheel, bulb garden wheel, garden calendar wheel, and a flowering houseplants garden wheel.

Grow It Gold Works (USA)
http://www.taoherbfarm.com
'Let our garden and landscape design computer software do your work for you.' You can create your own database and input the information you choose. With 7,000 plant records and 3,000 photos available, you can use the technology to refine your planning vision. The site includes a free slideshow demonstration.

Rebecca's Garden Planning (USA)
http://www.rebeccasgarden.com/planning
The web site is based on a syndicated weekly half-hour television series which offers gardening tips, informative how-to advice, and tours of inspirational gardens across the USA.

Society of Garden Designers
http://www.software-technics.co.uk/society-of-garden-designers
Affiliated to the RHS, the Society includes many household names among its members – authors of popular books on garden design, television gardening presenters, lecturers and tutors in garden design, and medal winners from the Chelsea and Hampton Court Palace Flower Shows and other national gardening exhibitions. The web site contains a list of full members, each with a description of their professional experience and the services they are offering. Some include plans and photographs of their work.

Fig. 61. The web site of the Society of Garden Designers in London tells you about the work of their members and how to contact them.

Bookmarks   Location: http://www.software-technics.co.uk/society-of-garden-designers/london.html   What's Relate

Society of Garden Designers - London

Affiliated to the Royal Horticultural Society

At a time when there are many people offering garden design and landscape design services, the Society of Garden Designers aims to provide the public, both in the UK and abroad, with the assurance of competence, quality, experience, and in the work of many members, outstanding artistic flair.

For the full index   **HOME**   go to the home page

Click here to view the terms of conditions on the use of the members list

Click here to view about engaging a member of the Society

7 Water and your garden

In this chapter we will explore:

▶ *water as a resource*

▶ *weeding and mulching*

▶ *water and your lawn*

▶ *planning for drought*

▶ *using recycled water*

▶ *water and pots, containers and hanging baskets*

▶ *water and the kitchen garden*

▶ *water and the flower garden*

▶ *wildlife and water*

▶ *water features in the garden*

▶ *maintaining ponds and water features*

. . . .

Water as a resource

Water is a very important aspect of gardening and gardens. It may be stating the obvious, but plants won't grow without it, and, with the exception of aquatic plants, may die if they get too much. In the UK we are very fortunate that our climate provides us with regular rainfall that does most of our watering for us. But at certain times of year, mainly in the late spring and summer, natural rainfall sometimes isn't enough. And with the prospect of global warming likely to make our summers drier, water becomes a scarce resource, and even more important in our gardens.

Fortunately, there's plenty we can do to give nature a helping hand. Most of the techniques covered are aimed at conserving as much water as we can rather than just turning on the kitchen tap. Using tap water and a hose pipe to water the garden may seem to be the easiest thing to do, but it certainly isn't particularly environmentally friendly, and may be impossible if a hose pipe ban is in force. Wise use of water in the garden is therefore a must.

Water Gardening in Texas
http://www.aggie-horticulture.tamu.edu/extension/homelandscape/watergarden
To see how arid areas manage to cope and to pick up some valuable hints, a visit to the web site Water Gardening in Texas is worthwhile. You will find some interesting information on xeriscaping (gardening in almost desert conditions).

Water and your garden..

Conserving water in the garden

According to the Environment Agency, a hosepipe uses on average 1100 litres of water an hour or 18.3 litres a minute, equivalent to about 122 two-gallon (9-litre) buckets. A sprinkler uses the same amount. A seep hose on average uses 100 litres an hour for every ten metre run. That's 11.1 of those two-gallon buckets. Imagine having to cart that lot down the garden! Well of course you wouldn't would you? And that's the point. Just switching off the tap and leaving the hose in the shed saves a great deal of water. But what about my plants, won't they all die if I don't water them? No, provided you have done a little planning beforehand.

Planning

This planning consists of working with nature rather than against. For example, growing drought resistant or drought tolerant plants, particularly in sunny spots such as south facing borders and beds, means you probably won't have to water at all. This saves you time and effort as well as conserving water supplies.

Making improvements to your soil so that it has a well-balanced structure means that plants are able to establish a deep and vigorous root system. Plants with a healthy root system are better able to cope with periods of drought. Adding lots of organic matter, such as well-rotted manure and home-made garden compost, will improve the structure of both sandy and clay soils and improve the drainage, as will digging in a commercially produced soil conditioner such as composted manure, and bark. Sandy soils retain more moisture throughout the year, and clay soils will become less waterlogged in winter and not turn to concrete in the summer. Compost and soil conditioners also help to feed the plants.

In a new garden it's worth taking the trouble to find out how much water each part of your garden may require. Do this by digging several holes about 25cm (10 inches) deep around the garden. Fill them with water and see how long the water takes to drain away. Where it drains quickly is the place to plant drought tolerant plants whilst the more water retentive areas are a good place for thirsty plants such as vegetables.

You also need to consider how sunny or windy the site is. In these areas plants lose more water by evaporation through their leaves than in sheltered sites. Trees and shrubs, hedging and climber covered trellis can be used to provide shelter from wind and sun.

What about established plants?

Once established, most trees, shrubs and perennials need little watering. Provided they are not allowed to go short of water in their first season or two they will put down a good root system and find their own water supply during drought periods. This is one good reason for planting container-grown plants during the warmer days of early autumn rather than during the summer. There is normally enough warmth left in the soil to get the plant away to a good start and rain is almost a certainty at that time of year. Keep a close eye on such transplants during the following spring and summer and water only when necessary to encourage a good root system and you can forget about having to water them in subsequent years.

Established plants should only need watering when they show signs of wilting and not before. Whilst this is a good rule of thumb to adopt, many plants will wilt during the heat of the day but perk up again overnight. This way the plant preserves its precious water resources. Too frequent watering, particularly with a hose, will encourage roots to grow to the surface and weaken the plant with possibly fatal results. It is better to use a watering can filled with rainwater and fitted with a spout. Direct the water to where the plant needs it – at the roots. Don't water the surrounding soil or the leaves, and water in the early morning or in the evening when it is cool. This avoids rapid evaporation of the water by hot sunshine.

Weeding and mulching

Two other techniques that help to conserve water are weeding and mulching around plant roots. This may seem like a lot of work, but if done at the right time, it actually saves time and effort. Removing weeds by hoeing or by hand makes sure that all available water reaches the roots of your plants and not the weeds. If after weeding you spread a mulch of well-rotted garden compost or manure, leaf mould, or composted bark over the soil surface and around your plants roots you will be suppressing weed growth and retaining moisture in the soil by slowing down evaporation. The mulch needs to be at least 2.5cm (1in) and not more than 7.5 cm (3ins) deep.

The best time to weed and mulch is when the soil is damp from rain. The weeds are easy to remove and there is plenty of moisture to be captured. Spring is a good time to do this whilst there is still some moisture left from winter rain. Most shrubs, trees and perennials will benefit from a feed at this time of year. So if you weed, feed and mulch at the same time you probably won't have to do anything else for another six months. And in the autumn, all you need do is remove any weeds and put down a new layer of mulch. Ordinary garden compost or leaf mould is fine for mulching in the autumn, but worm compost is the ideal for spring as it will feed, mulch and condition the soil all at the same time.

Southern Water
http://www.southernwater.co.uk
The web site for Southern Water has lots of tips and hints on the water

Fig. 62. Southern Water. The web site offers some expert tips and hints on the water-saving garden.

saving garden and is worth a visit. It also has a useful list of drought resistant plants.

Water and your lawn

Most of us admire a well-kept green lawn. Nothing seems to set off borders of summer flowers better. Unfortunately keeping them green throughout a long hot summer uses a huge amount of water. Keeping a sprinkler going for an hour a day for seven days uses enough water to fill 100 baths. Imagine what would happen if everyone down the road did the same thing. The local river could very soon dry up and we'd all be using stand-pipes.

Fortunately, watering the lawn isn't really necessary because grass is very resilient. Although it may turn brown and look as though it has died, a downpour of rain will soon turn it green again. And if the grass is mown less often during the summer and left to grow a little longer it will suffer less during rainless periods. Leaving the grass clippings on the surface during the summer helps retain moisture. Whilst spiking the lawn surface and raking in some fine compost in the autumn, improves drainage and allows moisture to reach the roots over the winter. A feed in spring and autumn encourages growth and root production, which makes the grass more drought resistant.

Planning for drought

If you are planning a new lawn, go for drought-resistant seeds strains or turf that consists of drought tolerant species. Alternatively, use ground cover plants instead of grass, and save yourself a lot of work by restricting the size of your lawn. If you have a large area to cover then consider a wild flower lawn using native wild flowers and grasses. This can be left for cutting until later in the summer after the plants have seeded themselves. A wild flower lawn will also attract birds, butterflies and other wildlife into your garden.

American Hometime
http://www.pbs.org/hometime/
An interesting site for information on lawns is the American Hometime web site. At the How-to Centre you will find many projects. Click on

Fig. 63. American Hometime includes information about successful lawn maintenance and watering.

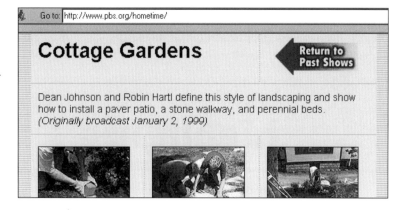

Lawn & Garden for information about making a lawn and lawn care including watering.

The Virtual Garden
http://www.vg.com
Another useful site for lawns is The Virtual Garden. You can find out just about anything to do with gardening here. And if you register you can get free access to a whole host of forums where you can air your views and pick up ideas and tips on different aspects of gardening. This site is vast. A search for ponds, for example, brings up a large number of interesting articles and features each of which you can click on and read. Click on the weekend projects link and discover all you ever wanted to know about water gardening.

Fig. 64. The Virtual Garden web site has a weekend projects link that will tell you lots about water gardening.

Using recycled water

In theory recycling bath, shower and water from laundry rinsing for use in your garden is a great idea. In practise collecting and storing this so-called 'grey' water is not quite so easy. The water needs to be siphoned into water buts using a hose and then you need somewhere to put all those containers.

A better idea might be to use a neat piece of equipment called a Rain Sava ('saver'). This diverts the rainwater falling on your roof from your downpipes to a water container or number of containers. Since the average house in the UK receives some 10,000 gallons of rain on its roof every year, that's a lot of water for free. In addition, this useful piece of kit can be used in conjunction with a hosepipe so that you can store this free water wherever you want it. And when your storage containers are full you can just shut the system off.

Shed and greenhouse roofs are also a good source of rainwater. Put up some guttering and a piece of pipe and divert the water into a water barrel. Keep a lid on the barrel to exclude light and prevent harmful organisms and algae from growing. One word of warning about rainwater: don't use it to water greenhouse seedlings in trays and pots. You could easily introduce diseases such as damping off and mildew into the compost. Only use clean tap water. That said, rainwater is perfectly safe for greenhouse plants once they are past the seedling stage, and is ideal for acid loving plants such as azaleas.

Water and pots, containers and hanging baskets

The compost in pots, containers and hanging baskets dries out much quicker than garden soil. During the summer most containers and baskets will need watering at least once a day, more often if they are in a sunny and windy spot. Small containers dry out more quickly than large ones so it makes sense to put a lot of plants into a large container rather than have lots of small ones to deal with.

Saving water

There are several water-saving techniques that can be used for containers and baskets. Use plastic pots rather than clay ones as these retain moisture better. Alternatively, if you don't like plastic pots, line clay ones with black plastic (a dustbin liner will do) before putting in the compost. But remember to leave the drainage hole in the bottom uncovered or the compost will become waterlogged and the plants will die.

Adding 'swell gel' to the compost will also help retain moisture and ensure that the compost doesn't dry out too quickly. A mulch of bark or gravel on the surface of the compost cuts down the evaporation and helps keep roots cool. It also helps prevent weeds from getting established in your containers and robbing the plants of vital food and moisture.

Hanging baskets also benefit from a moisture-retaining liner and the use of swell gel in the compost. Mulching the surface also helps reduce evaporation, but the mulch could get washed away when watering and gravel might make the baskets too heavy.

Water and the kitchen garden

Most vegetables thrive in sunny spots. Very few will tolerate heavy shade and produce a worthwhile crop. However, there are some crops that need very little water even in a dry summer. These include asparagus, beetroot, carrots, Jerusalem artichoke, leaf beet, onions, parsnip, rhubarb, shallots, sprouting broccoli, and turnip.

Most herbs like dry, light soils where there is good drainage and need sunshine to produce the best flavour. This makes them ideal for growing in pots and containers. The exception to this is mint, which grows best in a moist soil and will tolerate cool conditions and some shade. Nevertheless, mint should also be grown in a pot because it is very rampant and, given a chance, it will take over and become a nuisance. One way to contain it is to plant it in a large plastic pot and plunge the pot into the ground. This way the roots will remain moist and under control and you should not have to water it except in very dry conditions.

Some vegetables benefit from water at certain times. Potatoes and sweet corn should be watered as the fruit begins to swell. Broad beans and peas need water at the start of flowering and as the pods begin to swell. Courgettes benefit from water as the fruit begins to form. French beans shouldn't need watering at all. Just make sure the ground has a good soaking before you sow them.

Other crops need a constant supply of water throughout the growing season. These thirsty crops include most of the leaf vegetables such as lettuce, Chinese cabbage, cabbage, cauliflower, spinach, celery, leeks, cucumbers, tomatoes, radish and runner beans. These crops are best watered at the roots with a watering can on a regular basis unless there has been heavy rain and the soil is damp. Giving them a soaking twice or three times a week during dry weather is better than a trickle once a day.

When transplanting vegetables, particularly leaf crops like cabbage and lettuce, always soak the plants well before lifting or taking them out of their pots. Dig a hole where the plant is to go and fill it with water. Allow the water to drain away, spread out the roots in the hole and cover with soil. Leave a saucer shaped indent round the plant so that water will collect around the roots and not run off. Water well to the roots. If there is no rainfall, then these transplants will need watering regularly, preferably every day, for at least two weeks until they become established. Leaf vegetables will benefit from a soaking about three weeks before harvesting.

One labour-saving device is to plant vegetables with similar watering needs together, and to group the thirsty ones nearest to your water supply. Another useful technique is to grow vegetables through a plastic mulch or use a biodegradable membrane. This not only helps retain moisture but also cuts down weeds.

Fruits such as strawberries can also be grown through plastic. Alternatively a mulch of straw, composted bark or shredded paper will help keep the soil moist, reduce weeds, and deter slugs. Most fruit will yield a better crop if watered towards the end of flowering and as the fruit begins to swell. This is particularly true for strawberries and raspberries. If there is a dry spell at this time then water your fruit well; if not don't bother.

Water and the flower garden

Plants
Certain types of plants do particularly well in dry conditions. You can recognise many of them from their foliage. Cacti, sedums and succulents all have thick, fleshy leaves for storing water. Hairy leaves trap moisture; narrow curly or divided leaves reduce transpiration of water. Silver and grey leafed plants do particularly well in dry areas since the leaves reflect the heat. Many grey and silver foliaged plants are found growing in Mediterranean type climates. These make superb plants for gravel and Mediterranean gardens and for south-facing beds or borders, or any area that is dry but sunny.

Trees and shrubs
Planting trees and shrubs can provide shelter and shade for other plants. They can also provide interest throughout the year by way of colour, leaf

texture or structural form. Trees that like dry situations include arbutus unedo, the strawberry tree, cercis siliquastrum, the Judas tree, the bird cherry prunus padus pandora, and the Cockspur thorn *crataegus crus-galli*.

Many shrubs enjoy dry sunny positions. These include abelia, artemisia, berberis, ceanothus, cistus, genista, hebe, santolina, seneccio, yucca, and shrubby herbs such as lavender, rosemary, sage and thyme. Shrubs for dry shady sites include amelanchier, box, cotoneaster, euonymous, ivy, holly, mahonia, sambucus, skimmia. Some, such as berberis and cotoneaster, will grow just about anywhere except in waterlogged ground.

Dry-loving hardy perennials for sunny spots include acanthus, achillea, alstroemeria, dianthus, rock rose, poppy, penstemon, sedum. For shade try ajuga, alchemilla mollis (lady's mantle), bergenia, lamium, pulmonaria and vinca. There is a wide variety of hardy geranium species that are suitable for both shade and sun. Depending on their habit they can be grown to form clumps, to trail from pots and containers or to provide ground cover. Many hardy annuals will self-seed, which is useful if they come up where you want them to be, but a nuisance if you have to keep removing them. Transplant these when the weather and soil is damp to allow them to put down a good root system quickly.

Dry weather

The plants most vulnerable to dry conditions and drought are summer bedding plants. Many of them need to be planted in sunny positions to flower well and give a good show throughout the summer. Unfortunately many also suffer very quickly in hot, dry conditions. They may refuse to flower well, or worse, go to seed very quickly and stop flowering altogether. To overcome this, bedding plants need plenty of attention. Plant and forget is not really an option if you want a good summer display. You can cut the work of attending to bedding plants by getting them off to a good start.

Planting

Since the summer season is short, and bedding plants have only a few weeks to perform, only use healthy-looking well-grown stocky specimens. Small, weak and sickly plants will never do well and are a false economy. Don't plant too early as the soil will still be cold and you may get a late frost which could damage or kill the plants. If in doubt, warm the soil for a couple of weeks before planting, with a covering of black plastic. And keep some fleece handy to throw over the plants if frost is forecast.

Only plant when the soil is moist and use the technique of 'puddling' the plants in as described for vegetables. Incorporate some moisture retaining granules into the soil around the plants and mulch immediately after you have watered them in. This will lock in the water around the roots. Well-rotted garden compost, manure, composted bark or worm compost all make good mulches and will help to feed the plants.

New transplants will need regular watering until they are well established. A soaking three times a week is better than a trickle once a day.

This encourages them to put down a strong root system. Don't worry if they show signs of wilting soon after transplanting. As long as the soil is moist they should soon recover. Once established they should not require watering unless there is a dry period and the plants show signs of wilting, then a soaking two or three times a week is sufficient.

For bedding plants to do well throughout the summer they will need regular deadheading. Remove the flowers as they fade and don't allow them to produce seeds. This applies to almost all summer bedding plants, not just to plants like roses and sweet peas. They will also need regular feeding either by incorporating a general purpose fertiliser into the soil at planting time and again at six week intervals, or by using a liquid feed regularly throughout the summer. If you use a granular fertiliser and incorporate it into the soil, always water it in afterwards unless the soil is very moist. Plant roots cannot use the fertiliser unless it is first dissolved in water in the soil.

Aquamiser
http://www.garden-watering.com
For inexpensive labour and water saving devices that allow you to water the most vulnerable plants in your garden, that is pots, containers, annuals, bedding plants, seedlings and transplants in one go, visit the Aquamiser site. With this system you can hooked up a hose pipe to your tap, turn on the tap and have all your plants watered for you without lifting a watering can.

Wildlife and water

Providing drinking water in the garden – even if it is only a saucer full of water on the patio – will attract birds and other wildlife. Change the water frequently, because stagnant water attracts mosquitoes and midges. A more permanent water feature will not only attract wildlife but enhance the garden for its human inhabitants.

Fig. 65. Aquamiser is a supplier of inexpensive labour- and water-saving devices.

Water and your garden..

Water features in the garden

Many people feel a garden is incomplete without water. Certainly, no grand garden would be complete without its water feature, whether on the scale of the Palace of Versailles or something less dramatic like the waterlily pool in Monet's garden at Giverny. The desire to have water in the garden, no matter how small the area, has been fuelled by many popular television garden make-over programmes. A water feature has now become as necessary a part of a garden as a place to store the dustbins.

Water is visually very calming and cooling, and the sound of moving water can be a great stress reducer. However, before you rush out and dig up the lawn to put in a pond, give the idea some careful thought, and ask yourself some questions.

For example, why do you want water in your garden? Is it because you find the idea of sitting beside a pool on a hot summer evening sipping a glass of wine, attractive? Or do you want to bring wildlife into the garden? There may be many reasons, which should determine the kind of water feature you decide on. If it's for sitting beside, then a formal pool with fish may be what you need. If it's for wildlife then something more natural will be required.

Another question is: Where will you site the water feature? If it is to be a pond then position it in a reasonably sunny part of the garden where it gets at least six hours' sunshine a day. Keep it away from any overhanging trees or shrubs. Wildlife ponds can be placed in shadier spots where nearby shrubs and trees will provide cover and protection from predators. If you want moving water, you will need a pump and an electricity supply. This means running an electric cable from your house to your pump. Consult a qualified electrician about the best way to do this.

Royal Society for the Prevention of Accidents
http://www.rospa.co.uk
The subject of safety is another consideration. The ROSPA site offers some useful advice and contains some sobering statistics. If you have young children, particularly very young ones, then a pond is probably not a good idea. According to the Society, nine children drowned in garden ponds in the UK last year. If you have young children, a pebble fountain would be a safer alternative.

Pebble fountains can provide the sensual stimulus of moving water without a potentially dangerous open body of water. The water tank containing the pump is sunk into the ground just below soil level. The tank is covered with a metal grid through which the fountain projects. Large pebbles are placed on the grid. The water then splashes onto the pebbles and drains back into the underground tank, from where it is circulated back to the fountain by the pump. The fountain can be adjusted to provide a trickle or a jet. The same idea can be used for wall fountains where the water circulates through a plastic pipe leading to a wall mask. Pebble fountains can be used as a feature in bog gardens where the soil remains permanently moist. Many attractive plants will grow in this situa-

RoSPA

Index

About RoSPA

What's New

The Royal Society for the Prevention of Accidents

"RoSPA's purpose is to enhance the quality of life by exercising a powerful influen accident prevention"

tion. Some require sun while others will tolerate shade. To create a bog garden, remove 20 to 25cms (8 to 10ins) of soil, line the area with black plastic pierced with some drainage holes, and replace the soil. The drainage holes are needed to let the build up of water slowly drain away, otherwise the area will become waterlogged and stagnant, and nothing will survive.

Fig. 66. The web site of the Royal Society for the Prevention of Accidents.

In shady areas the bog garden will probably remain moist all year round. In sunny spots it may well dry out in summer and could require watering to keep the soil moist. Use rainwater for this, because tap water, which is normally alkaline, may upset the pH balance of the soil.

Maintaining ponds and water features

All ponds and water features require regular maintenance. Formal pools with fish are probably the most demanding, and pebble fountains the least. Wildlife ponds come somewhere in between. All ponds and water features need topping up from time to time, particularly in summer when water evaporation is at its highest. They will need to be kept clean and free from algae and pond weed. Use a rake or a net to remove debris and unwanted plants. Autumn is a good time for maintenance. Fallen leaves can be removed. If allowed to remain in the water they will decompose and the nitrogen released into the water will encourage algae to grow.

After filling, ponds take some time to settle down and establish a balanced ecosystem. A pond that is out of balance will go green. This indicates a lack of oxygen and excessive nitrogen in the water. Make sure there are enough oxygenating plants in the water, and that you have a good balance between deeper water and marginal plants. This helps to keep the water rich in oxygen, which discourages algae. Fountains also help to oxygenate water but should not be used in wildlife ponds.

Ponds made specifically to provide a habitat for wildlife should be still. Pond insects and amphibians do not live in moving water. Nor should such ponds have fish introduced to them. The fish will eat all the insects and any spawn laid by frogs, toads or newts. When you come to choose plants for this type of pond go for native species. Buy these from a reputable dealer or water garden specialist. Do not take them from the wild – it's illegal and damaging to the natural environment. Make sure you do not introduce some of the more rampant types of water plants to your pond. Go to a specialist water garden centre and ask them to recommend a selection of non-invasive plants and native species.

Fig. 67. The web site of the International Waterlily and Water Gardening Society.

International Waterlily and Water Gardening Society
http://www.iwgs.org.
This is a useful site for information on waterlilies and other water gardening information with links to other useful sites.

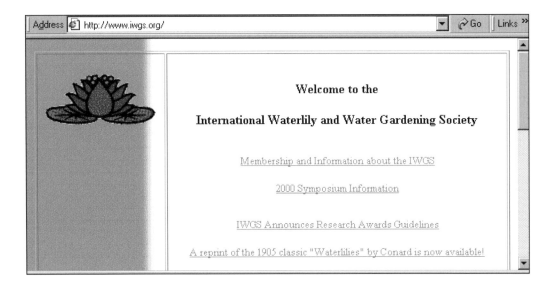

| Address | http://www.iwgs.org/ | ▼ | ⌀ Go | Links » |

Welcome to the

International Waterlily and Water Gardening Society

Membership and Information about the IWGS

2000 Symposium Information

IWGS Announces Research Awards Guidelines

A reprint of the 1905 classic "Waterlilies" by Conard is now available!

8 Annual gardening shows

In this chapter we will explore:

▶ *online calendars of gardening shows*
▶ *events from January to December*

. . . .

Online calendars of gardening shows

This chapter offers a monthly listing of some well-known annual garden-ing shows for which there are web sites. The web sites contain details of dates and events. How about planning a touring holiday? You can link the details given here with the details on famous gardens and on gardening holidays later in this book. You can then visit some superb gardens, going on to visit a show being held in the area.

GardenWeb's Calendar of Garden Events
http://www.gardencalendar.com
This useful online calendar lists worldwide events as submitted by garden clubs, plant societies, botanical gardens and others holding garden-related events. This web page (figure 68) lists garden events in date order. You can display the listings by date, location, type of event and/or keyword, or use the on-screen form provided. If you would like to add an event to the calendar, there is an online submission form.

Fig. 68. Garden Calendar is a very handy online source of details of forthcoming horticultural events and shows all over the world. There are hyperlinks which take you to more detailed information about each event.

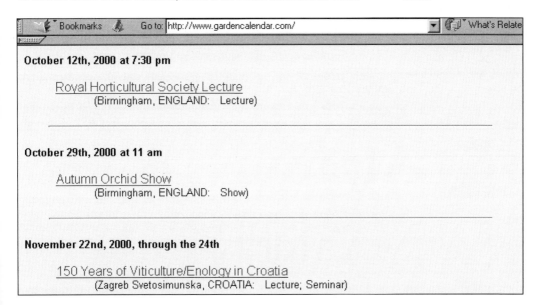

UK Horticultural Trade Show Calendar
http://www.ukexnet.co.uk/hort/cha/showuk.htm
This is a very useful resource. It sets out the names of the events, dates,

venues, contact names of the organisers, telephone and fax numbers (but not web sites). The calendar is maintained by the UKexnet Horticultural Index.

International Horticultural Trade Show Calendar 2000
http://www.ukexnet.co.uk/hort/cha/showint.htm
This detailed calendar of the major international shows is also maintained by the UKexnet Horticultural Index (see above).

The entries for gardening shows listed below are in normal date order. Check with the various organisations for the actual dates and venues. Please note that this information is liable to change. For particular events not listed here, remember to use your favourite search engine. We have included a number of overseas events as well.

January

Hortiflor
http://www.salons-online.com/approche/hortiflor.html
Hortiflor is the annual horticultural flowers exhibition held in Paris, France. It takes place at the Paris Expo, Porte de Versailles.

Royal Horticultural Society Flower Show
http://www.rhs.org.uk
Venue: the RHS Horticultural Halls in central London. This is a two-day monthly show. Botanical art is featured as well as displays from top nurseries. See the web site for the show calendar.

February

Fig. 69. The Alpine Garden Society web site contains detailed information about its shows.

Alpine Garden Society Non-Competitive Display
http://www.alpinegardensociety.org
Venue: Caerleon College, Caerleon, UK.

Alpine Garden Society Non-Competitive Display
http://www.alpinegardensociety.org
Venue: Burleigh College Thorpe Hill Loughborough, UK.

International Plant Fair
http://www.sna.org/programs/ipm/ipm.html
IPM is the International Plant Fair held in Essen, Germany. More than 1,200 exhibitors from 35 nations show their products to more than 54,000 trade buyers. National pavilions from Holland, Spain, Italy, Britain and the US show such products as trees, flowering plants, flowers, seeds, seedlings, bulbs and more.

RHS Flower Show
http://www.rhs.org.uk
Venue: the RHS Horticultural Halls, Westminster, London. It is a two-day show. Botanic art is featured as well as displays from top nurseries.

Fig. 70. The Royal Horticultural Society's web site events page.

March

Alpine Garden Society Early Spring Show
http://www.alpinegardensociety.org
Venue: Harlow, Essex, UK. It takes place on the first Saturday in March (figure 69).

Chicago Flower and Garden Show
http://www.chicagoflower.com
This is an annual event held at Chicago's Navy Pier. It features exhibits, gardening seminars, children's activities and shopping.

Daffodil Weekend
Email: church.wch@rednet.co.uk
Venue: Methodist Central Hall, Westminster, London.

Annual gardening shows ....

East Lancashire Show Alpine Garden Society
http://www.alpinegardensociety.org
Venue: Tottington High School, Laurel Street, Tottington, UK.

Kent Show Alpine Garden Society
http://www.alpinegardensociety.org
Venue: Rainham School for Girls Highfield Road, Rainham, Gillingham, UK.

Loughborough Show Alpine Garden Society
http://www.alpinegardensociety.org
Venue: Burleigh Community College, Thorpe Hill, Loughborough, UK.

Morecambe Show Alpine Garden Society
http://www.alpinegardensociety.org
Venue: Lancaster and Morecambe College, Morecambe Road, Lancaster, UK.

Fig. 71. Held in Massachusetts, the New England Spring Flower Show is a key date in the calendar for gardeners in the USA.

New England Spring Flower Show
http://www.masshort.org
The event brings the warmth and colour of springtime to Boston in Massachusetts, and over 150,000 visitors each year.

Philadelphia Flower Show
http://www.libertynet.org/flowrsho
Started in 1829, this is the largest (33 acres) annual indoor flower show in the world, and the oldest flower show in the United States. Some 285,000 visitors attended in 2000.

RHS Orchid Show
http://www.rhs.org.uk
Venue: the RHS Horticultural Halls, Westminster, London. This is a two-day show featuring orchid displays from some of the top nurseries and growers.

RHS Early Spring Show
http://www.rhs.org.uk
Venue: the RHS Horticultural Halls, Westminster, London. This two-day show features spring flowers, camellias, rhododendrons, azaleas, daffodils and ornamental plants.

Royal National Rose Society Spring Garden Care Weekend
http://www.roses.co.uk
Venue: St Albans, Hertfordshire, UK.

San Francisco Garden Show
http://www.gardenshow.com/sf/index.html
Venue: the show is held in mid March at the Cow Palace in San Francisco, USA.

April

Cleveland Show – Alpine Society
http://www.alpinegardensociety.org
Venue: Ian Ramsey Church of England School, Green's Lane, Fairfield, Stockton-on-Tees, UK.

Dublin Show – Alpine Garden Society
http://www.alpinegardensociety.org
Venue: Cabinteely Community School, Co. Dublin, Ireland.

London Show – Alpine Garden Society
http://www.alpinegardensociety.org
Venue: the RHS Old Hall, Vincent Square, Westminster, London.

Melbourne International Flower & Garden Show
http://www.melbflowershow.com.au
The Melbourne International Flower and Garden Show is one of Australia's most beautiful events, representing all areas of the ornamental horticulture industry. It is held each year within the historic and beautifully restored Royal Exhibition Building. Over the last four years 500,000 visitors have attended the event.

Midland Show – Alpine Garden Society
http://www.alpinegardensociety.org
Venue: Alderbrook School, Blossomfield Road, Solihull, West Midlands, UK.

North Midland Show – Alpine Garden Society
http://www.alpinegardensociety.org

Venue: Brookfield School, Chatsworth Road, Chesterfield, UK.

North of England – Alpine Garden Society Show
http://www.alpinegardensociety.org
Venue: the Great Yorkshire Showground, Harrogate, UK.

Northumberland Show – Alpine Garden Society/Scottish Rock Garden Club
http://www.alpinegardensociety.org
Venue: the Wentworth Leisure Centre, Hexham, Northumberland, UK.

RHS Spring Show
http://www.rhs.org.uk
Venue: the Horticultural Halls, Westminster, London. Spring flowering plants including rhododendrons, daffodils, tulips and ornamental plants. Daffodil Show. Also camellias and ornamental plants.

South West Show – Alpine Garden Society
http://www.alpinegardensociety.org
Venue: St Thomas School, Hatherleigh, Exeter, Devon, UK.

Ulster Show – Alpine Garden Society
http://www.alpinegardensociety.org
Venue: Muckamore, Antrim, Northern Ireland.

May

Chelsea Flower Show
http://www.rhs.org.uk
Venue: The Royal Hospital, Chelsea, London. This is the premier show of the year in the UK. Admission is by ticket only. You will need to book well in advance to be sure of getting in.

East Anglia Show – Alpine Garden Society
http://www.alpinegardensociety.org
Venue: Wymondham College, Wymondham, Norfolk, UK.

East Cheshire Show Alpine Garden Society
http://www.alpinegardensociety.org
Venue: Macclesfield College, Park Lane, Macclesfield, UK.

Holker Garden Festival
http://www.btinternet.com/~lake.district/sl/holker.htm
Venue: Holker Hall and Gardens, Cark-in-Cartmel, Grange-over-Sands, Cumbria, UK.

Malvern Show – Alpine Garden Society
http://www.alpinegardensociety.org
Venue: the Three Counties Showground, Malvern, Worcestershire, UK.

Southport Show – Alpine Garden Society
http://www.alpinegardensociety.org
Venue: Lord Street South Church Hall, Southport, Lancashire, UK.

June

BBC Gardeners' World Live
http:/gardenersworld.beeb.htm
Venue: National Exhibition Centre (NEC), Birmingham, UK. See the BBC *Gardeners World* web site for dates and further details.

Cleveland Botanical Garden Flower Show
http://www.cbgarden.org
Cleveland Botanical Garden in Ohio hosts the largest annual outdoor flower show in North America.

North Summer Show – Alpine Garden Society
http://www.alpinegardensociety.org
Venue: Pudsey Civic Hall, Dawson's Corner, Pudsey, West Yorkshire, UK.

RHS Summer Show
http://www.rhs.org.uk
Venue: the Horticultural Halls, Westminster, London. This month's show is ornamental plants.

South Summer Show – Alpine Garden Society
http://www.alpinegardensociety.org
Venue: Merrist Wood Agricultural College, Worplesdon, Guildford, Surrey, UK.

July

Cheltenham Show – Alpine Garden Society
http://www.alpinegardensociety.org
Venue: Pittville School, Albert Road, Cheltenham, UK.

Hampton Court Palace and Flower Show
http://www.sisley.co.uk/hamptnct.htm
This show is a delight and a rival to Chelsea. This particular site illustrates a tour to the Show organised by Sisley.

RHS Flower Show
http://www.rhs.org.uk
Venue: Tatton Park, UK. See the RHS Web site for details.

RHS Flower Show
http://www.rhs.org.uk
Venue: Horticultural Halls, Westminster, London. The monthly two-day show.

Wisley Flower Show
http://www.rhs.org.uk
Venue: the RHS Garden at Wisley near Woking, Surrey, UK.

Address http://www.battleofflowers.com/

Welcome to the Jersey Battle of Flowers

The floral Battle Parade and the illuminated Moonlight Parade are the largest and most popular events in the Jersey tourism calendar. They bring together the Island's community in the organisation and preparation of magnificent

Fig. 72. The Jersey Battle of Flowers has its own web site here.

August

Battle of Flowers
http://www.battleofflowers.com/
Venue: St Helier, Jersey, Channel Islands. This floral Battle Parade and the illuminated Moonlight Parade are the largest and most popular events in the Jersey tourism calendar. This is a spectacular parade of flower-covered floats through the streets.

Plantarium
http://www.plantarium.nl
Held in Boskoop, Holland, this is a leading international tree and horticultural event. Some 250 participants from many different countries present a collection of nursery stock for the consumer market. Containers and plant pots for nursery stock are on display, as are plants for growing in the soil.

RHS Summer Flower Show
http://www.rhs.org.uk
Venue: the Horticultural Halls, Westminster, London. This month it is gladioli and ornamental plants, plus an exhibition of botanical photographs.

Southport Flower Show
http://www.theflowershow.free.online.co.uk
Venue: the Victoria Park Showground, Southport, Lancashire, UK.

September

Flormart
http://www.padovafiere.it/fiere/flormart
This is a popular floricultural exhibition held in Padova in Italy, attracting over 30,000 visitors each year.

Harrogate's Autumn Flower Show
http://www.flowershow.org.uk/autumn
The show is organised by the North of England Horticultural Society at the Great Yorkshire Showground, Harrogate, North Yorkshire, UK.

Hobart Horticultural Society
http://www.tased.edu.au/tasonline/hobhort
Based in the capital of Tasmania, Australia, this society holds four flower shows each year, two in spring and two in autumn.

Hortimat
http://www.jarditec.com
Hortimate is a Paris-based international show for horticultural equipment, materials and production. There are around 1,000 exhibitors, attracting over 62,000 visitors.

Malvern Autumn Show
http://www.rhs.org.uk/Around/shows/malvaut.asp
Venue: the Three Counties Showground, Malvern, Worcestershire, UK.

Newcastle Show – Alpine Garden Society
http://www.alpinegardensociety.org
Venue: the Memorial Hall, Darras Road, Ponteland, Newcastle-upon-Tyne, UK.

RHS Great Autumn Show
http://www.rhs.org.uk
Venue: the Horticultural Halls, Westminster, London, UK.

Wirral Show – Alpine Garden Society
http://www.alpinegardensociety.org
Venue: Christleton High School, Village Road, Christleton, Chester, UK.

October

RHS Autumn Show.
http://www.rhs.org.uk
Venue: the Horticultural Halls, Westminster, London. This month it's autumn fruit and vegetables, and ornamental plants.

Sussex Show – Alpine Garden Society
http://www.alpinegardensociety.org
Venue: Tanbridge House School, Guildford Road, Horsham, West Sussex, UK.

Annual gardening shows ....

November

RHS Autumn Flower Show
http://www.rhs.org.uk
Venue: Horticultural Halls, Westminster, London, UK. The show features ornamental plants, apples and pears, and an exhibition of botanical paintings.

RHS Late Autumn Show
http://www.rhs.org.uk
Venue: Horticultural Halls, Westminster, London, UK. Ornamental plants and botanical paintings feature at this show.

December

RHS Christmas Show
http://www.rhs.org.uk
Venue: Horticultural Halls, Westminster, London, UK – the last big show of the year.

9 Gardening holidays & courses

In this chapter we will explore:

▶ *choosing a garden-based holiday*

▶ *holidays in the UK and Ireland*

▶ *holidays in Europe*

▶ *worldwide holidays*

▶ *gardening courses*

. . . .

Choosing a garden-based holiday

There are lots of opportunities to see some fantastic gardens and to give yourself some real treats along the way. You could read this chapter in connection with the diary dates in chapter 8, and the final chapter that deals with 'celebrity gardening'. This should generate plenty of ideas for worthwhile and memorable garden-based holidays.

This chapter includes details of organised coach trips where you can join like-minded gardeners on an organised trip. It also includes gardens that are worthy of a visit for their sheer beauty. A good plan is to select one area of the country and arrange your own tour to take in a number of the gardens in that area.

Holidays in the UK and Ireland

All Seasons Theme Tours: Gardens
http://www.allseasons.demon.co.uk/gardens.htm
The tour by minibus covers 21 gardens including such internationally famous ones as Sissinghurst, Exbury, Leonardslee, Heligan Manor, and Great Dixter. Another option for touring some beautiful gardens, if your pocket is deep enough, is to have your own private guide on a chauffeur-driven tour. Actually, it is not too expensive, the vehicle being a 7-seater Renault Espace.

Barnsley House Garden – Rosemary Verey's Garden (Sisley Tours)
http://www.tka.co.uk/sisley/barnsley.htm
This Sisley tour includes Rosemary Verey's garden at Barnsley House. The garden is set in the Cotswolds and was featured as part of her television series. The garden itself is no more than three acres and is a wonderful inspiration for projects on a smaller scale. The Prince of Wales is quoted here as saying: 'Mrs Verey makes gardening seem the easiest and most natural thing in the world.' You can also view the following web site (figure 73) for more about Mrs Verey's garden: http://www.cotswolds-calling.com/houses-gardens/barnsley.htm

Gardening holidays & courses ....

Fig. 73. Rosemary Verey's garden at Barnsley House in the English Cotswolds.

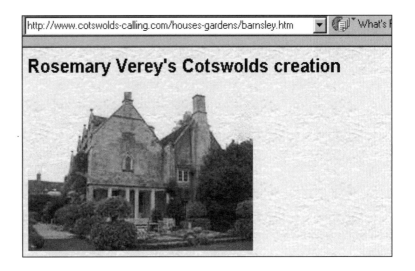

Chelsea Flower Show and Hampton Court Flower Show (Blue Chip Travel)
http://www.bluechiptravel.co.uk
Blue Chip runs trips to these shows (reservations: 0131 226 6157).

Christopher Lloyd's Garden
http://www.sissons.demon.co.uk/dixter.htm
This is another tour site. It contains details of Christopher Lloyd's garden at Great Dixter. Lloyd writes regularly for the newspapers and magazines. He has developed some enchanting cottage garden effects.

Destination Europe – English Gardens
http://www.heartofeurope.com/itinchel.html
Destination Europe offers a tightly packed programme of tours to Chelsea, Sissinghurst, and lots of other famous gardens. The vagaries of the British weather mean that a particular garden may or may not be open, so the itinerary may be flexible. With dollar pricing on the web site, they are clearly aiming at the US market.

Fig. 74. Destination Europe offers a large programme of garden-related tours.

F L O R A Garden Tours

F L O R A Garden Tours take you to the finest gardens in Britain. As well as the famous gardens the tours visit lesser known but lovely ones, some rarely open to the public. The tour director and leader is <u>Dr Barbara Sommerville</u>, a biologist of international repute who has a deep interest in the history of gardening, landscape and architecture.

New: Click **here** for a **F L O R A** traveller's diary of a tour including the Hampton Court flower show in 1999.

Tours of Cambridge Gardens

The <u>Cambridge based garden tours</u> stay in spacious accommodation in magnificent old colleges. They last five days and tour on foot and by coach with slide-talks or exhibitions each evening. Click on the section heading for tour dates.

Flora Garden Tours: Guided Tours of Gardens in England
http://www.cam.net.uk/home/aaa217
This tour involves a stay in Glastonbury, famous as the home of ancient legends and alternative therapies. The trip includes a visit to Hestercombe, a developing garden in which you can see all of the hard work that has gone on, and what is planned for the future. The trip then goes on to take in Rosemoor, the Royal Horticultural Society Garden in Devon. The wheelchair access is excellent. Flora offers many other tours around the UK: take a look at their web site (figure 75) and see for yourself.

Fig. 75. Flora Garden Tours offers guided tours of some of the best-known gardens in England.

Garden Tours
http://www.gardentours.com/
This is an established American company that offers tours to a number of different gardens in the UK. The service appeared to be partly suspended in 2000.

Garden Tours for Connoisseurs (About Travel)
http://www.aboutravel.com/spring02.html
This site has a section called Garden Tours of Europe, including one where you can meet Rosemary Verey at Barnsley House. When we viewed the site some out-of-date tours remained listed. They run some trips to some wonderful Scottish gardens, for instance: 'The flowers of Scotland, the grand gardens of Edinburgh and Aberdeen; Edzell Castle and Crathes, Pitmeddon Garden and the romantic ruins of Kildrummy; the Grampian Highlands, Scone Palace and St Andrews. Lovely, wistful and Celtic.'

Geoff Hamilton's Barnsdale Garden (Blue Chip Travel)
http://www.bluechiptravel.co.uk
Blue Chip Travel has a package called 'The Best of British Heritage', which contains the trip to Barnsdale. Here you will be able to see the model gardens and themed areas, in particular the kitchen ornamental garden

made for the television series of the same name, and two gardens created for the series *Paradise Gardens*. You also get a trip to Sandringham, the country home of the Royal Family in Norfolk. There are sixty acres of grounds with two lakes, streams and woodland walks to enjoy. The package includes a trip to Norfolk Lavender, the last full lavender farm in England, with gardens of lavender, herbs and roses. You can learn all about the distillation and oil production of the lavender scent.

Helicopter Trip to the Isles of Scilly (Travelsphere)
http://www.travelsphere.co.uk
This trip by Travelsphere includes a guided tour of the famous Abbey Gardens, Tresco. The environment is such that sub-tropical plants can be grown here. If you buy plants on the island, be sure you know how to look after them when you return home. The helicopter ride is obviously quicker than the ferry and may save you getting seasick.

Hidden Gardens of Ireland (Garden Tours)
http://www.gardentours.com/IrelandHiddenG.htm
According to the web site (figure 76) they run tours to: Muckross House and Gardens, Ring of Kerry Tour, Inacullin on Garinish Island, Mount Congreve Mahaffey House, Powerscourt Ballymaloe, Lodge Park Walled Garden, Ballynacourty National Botanic Gardens, Graigueconna, Brown Private Garden; Glendalough, Fairfield Lodge, Mallahide Castle, Lakernount Gardens, Kaduna, Dunloe Castle, Wicklow Gardens Festival; Blarney Woollen Mills, Helen Dillon Garden, Iveragh Peninsula; Dunloe Castle, Ram House, Primrose Hill, Blarney Castle, Butterstream – the home of the Blarney stone. The Blarney stone is located at the top of the castle and involves a real bend down backwards to kiss it. It is not accessible for people who are wheelchair bound but there is still the magic of the castle itself.

Fig. 76. Hidden Gardens of Ireland is one of the trips on offer from GardenTours.com.

FARMING   GARDENS   SPORTS   CRUISES

WELCOME to Arena / RHS 2000 Garden Holidays

Bookmark this page as we will update it with the very latest bargain garden tour offers.

SCROLL DOWN or GO STRAIGHT TO A FEATURED TOUR:

Click the ● to return to the top of this page

Friday, June 02, 2000

Visit the RHS Home Page for details of membership and other offers

NEW ONLINE RESERVATION

- Giverny & Normandy Gardens
- Gardens of Japan
- Vineyards & Gardens of Alsace & the Black Forest
- Courson Autumn Show & Giverny

Arena/RHS Holidays
http://www.arenatravel.com/gardens.htm
The Arena Travel site is well worth bookmarking, since its holidays are arranged for the Royal Horticultural Society. It has some wonderful holidays on offer, in fact they look so tempting that we are considering booking one ourselves. There is an online reservation form, and you can send off for a brochure. You can make contact with them by email, fax, post, telephone or internet form. All its holidays are tailor made, so if you wish to arrange a holiday for your own group you can contact their Business Development Manager for further details.

Fig. 77. The Arena Travel service is a must for tour information.

Wallace Arnold Holidays
http://www.wallacearnold.com
Wallace Arnold offers holidays for gardeners all over the UK, including to Yorkshire, Warwick, Derby, Leicester, Devon and Dorset. The holidays involve stays in quality hotels, and the ever popular pub lunch. The company employs some well-known gardeners to lead its trips, so you could well find a 'name' on the coach, someone with local knowledge and local contacts. They sometimes take parties to delightful small out of the way gardens that members of the public would not normally be able to access.

Holidays in Europe

Dutch Bulbfields (Travelsphere)
http://www.travelsphere.co.uk
The company offers a range of short coach and air tours which include the Dutch bulbfields.

Le Jardin des Cinq Sens
http://www.geneve-tourisme.ch/fr/decouvrir.html
We discovered 'the Garden of the Five Senses' in 1997 when we visited the French Alps. It is a delight. It is about 20 minutes away from Geneva

on the lakeside at Yvoire, a charming medieval village. After we had toured the garden we encountered the baron and his wife. We did not introduce ourselves as writers until we had finished seeing the gardens. What we saw was superb. The gardens include The Garden of Taste, The Perfume Garden, The Garden of Texture, The Garden of Colour and The Garden of Hearing. Each one has a theme representing a particular sense. The Garden of Hearing, for example, contains aviaries of twittering birds, and the sound of running water. The Garden of Colours offers a superb show of colour – iris, lilacs and geraniums. The gardens are so successful at stimulating the senses that brain-damaged children are brought here on special trips.

Le Jardin Secret
http://www.digicom.qc.ca/fleurdelotus/index.htm
The 'Secret Garden' is very much an artist's garden, and has been the passion of a family for some years. The garden itself is at Annency, about two hours from Geneva in the French Alps. We stayed in Megeve and visited this garden. The site of course is in French. Visiting the garden was a remarkable experience. You could take in Le Jardin des Cinq Sens (above) and this garden on the same trip.

New Gardens of Northern Europe (Travelsphere)
http://www.travelsphere.co.uk
This is a four-day trip sold as a long weekend. It takes in some of the best gardens in the Netherlands, Germany and Belgium. These include the gardens at Kerkrade, the Cologne Botanic Gardens, and the National Botanic Gardens at Brussels.

Worldwide holidays

Fig. 78. Canadian Gardening Online offers an annual programme of worldwide holidays.

Canadian Gardening Online
http://canadiangardening.com
The company runs a variety of garden-based tours. Examples include the gardens and hilltop towns of Tuscany, gardens of the Atlantic coastal

plain, and a Pacific Northwest garden tour (figure 78). The site also includes some discussion groups called Garden Talk, where you can log on and compare notes with other gardeners about a wide range of topics.

Gardening courses

The development of the internet makes it possible for people to study horticulture anywhere in the world. There is not space to list everything available, but here are some of the courses that have caught our attention. Some are residential, others are courses that you can either follow as traditional distance-learning courses, or online via the internet.

Ashfield College
http://www.ashfield-college.com/adult/gardening.htm
Ashfield College near Dublin offers a range of gardening and flower-arranging courses (figure 79). The college is in a residential area, on the main bus routes but away from city centre distractions.

Fig. 79. Ashfield College in Dublin runs a variety of floristry and gardening courses.

Backyard Nature
http://www.backyardnature.com
Some informal online courses (figure 80) are run by an American publishing organisation. 'Learn how to attract your favorite birds and wildlife to your own backyard by taking innovative, self-paced online courses. These online training courses are fun, informative, and practical. They will help you learn about nature, the environment, birds, wildlife, and backyard landscaping, gardening and native plants.'

Gardening holidays & courses ....

Fig. 80. Backyard Nature
is developing some
gardening courses online.

Address: http://www.backyardnature.com/exec/gt/new_online_courses.html

Learn about backyard wildlife and gardening with online courses

Soon you will be able to learn how to attract your favorite birds and wildlife to your own backyard by taking innovative, self paced online courses. These online training courses are fun, informative, and practical. They will help you learn about nature, the environment, birds, wildlife, and backyard landscaping, gardening and native plants.

Some of the online courses we are developing include:

Backyard Wildlife

- Attracting birds with habitat
- Get rid of pests effectively
- Appreciate squirrels...and keep them out of your birdfeeders

Fig. 80. Backyard Nature is developing some gardening courses online.

Berkshire College of Agriculture
http://www.berks-coll-ag.ac.uk/cpart.htm
Berkshire College in Reading, Berkshire, offers a number of interesting part-time courses on floristry, flower arrangement, forestry and arboriculture, chainsaw competence, Royal Forestry Society certificate, gardening short courses and workshops

Centre for Holistic Living
http://ds.dial.pipex.com/town/estate/kaa46
This organisation has grounds in south-west Wales and runs various courses that reflect its philosophy. With their organic gardens, a stay here could be worth considering.

English Gardening School
http://www.englishgardeningschool.co.uk
Based at the Chelsea Physic Garden in the heart of London, this is a delightful provider of distance learning courses (figure 81). The idea of an art course that includes the element of time is specially appealing. 'Discover us within London's secret garden… part-time intensive learning, inspirational tutors, the widest range of gardening and related subjects, distance learning and garden tours.'

Fig. 81. The English Gardening School is held at the Chelsea Physic Garden in central London.

Address: http://www.englishgardeningschool.co.uk/   Go   Links »

The English Gardening School

AT THE CHELSEA PHYSIC GARDEN, LONDON

Discover us within London's 'Secret Garden'...
part time intensive learning,
inspirational tutors,
the widest range of gardening and related subjects,
distance learning and garden tours.

Contact   One Year Courses
About the School   Short Courses
Applying for a Course   Summer School

Gardening and Horticulture Courses
http://www.acs.edu.au/hort
Gardening and horticulture courses from Australia are available here. They form part of the Australian Correspondence Schools network and offer a number of interesting courses.

Gardening UK
http://www.gardening-uk.co.uk/training.htm
The UK generally is not nearly as well represented on the internet as the USA, but things are beginning to change. Good courses are available, and a worthwhile listing of UK institutions and organisations offering courses of various kinds can be found here. This is quite an extensive list (figure 82), although a number of these organisations are not yet on the web. How much longer can they afford to wait?

Fig. 82. Gardening UK provides a useful online listing of horticultural courses.

Horticultural Correspondence College, Wiltshire
mailto:hc.college@btinternet.com
The college offers flexible home study for the RHS General Exam in Horticulture. You can study garden design, organic gardening, herbs and conservation. You can email them for a prospectus.

Institute of Garden Design
http://ds.dial.pipex.com/institute/gd.htm
The IGD offers a Diploma in Garden Design available by home study. The Institute's tutors are full-time garden designers. The web site contains course details, an online application form, and garden design tips. This independent service is based near Wedmore in Somerset, and is listed in the Learning Direct database of the UK Department for Education.

KLC School of Design
http://www.klc.co.uk/
Established for 20 years, KLC is a leading educational establishment for professional and personal training, and offers full-time, part-time and home study courses in both interior and garden design. Students can choose to undertake a vocational training for entry into either industry, or simply develop the necessary skills to take a more professional approach to their own home or garden projects. The school is based at Chelsea Harbour, London.

Gardening holidays & courses ....

Oxford College of Garden Design
http://www.ocgd.demon.co.uk
The College was founded in 1992 with the aim of producing Britain's top future designers and to fulfil students' design potential. It has the bonus of being validated by Oxford Brookes University. Its one-year course is a linear course with ongoing evaluation over four terms – three academic terms starting in October and ending in June, with the summer term June to September based on home study projects. Design projects make up 50% of the possible marks, project work accounts for 40% and a final exam in June makes up the final 10%. The College is based at Henley-on-Thames in Oxfordshire.

Regent Academy
http://www.regentacademy.com
Based in London, the Regent Academy runs a large programme of home study courses.

Workshops Arts and Artists
http://www.southfrance.com/workshopindex.html#verger
This one may seem to have little to do with gardening, but it does offer gardening courses in a French environment. 'Enjoy one of the many six day courses held at a beautiful chateau. Courses include watercolour painting, sculpture and moulding, portraiture and drawing, dance, photography, *trompe l'oeil*, special paint effects, gardening techniques and planning.' If you are keen on combining gardening and art, this could be just the thing for you.

Writtle College
http://www.writtle.ac.uk/
This is a Chelmsford-based college of further and higher education which runs a variety of undergraduate and postgraduate courses. However, it also offers quite a big selection of short courses on everything from creating rock and water gardens, to propagation workshops, landscaping, pest control, and carnivorous plants. It organises some events for the nearby RHS Hyde Hall garden.

Wye College, University of London
http://www.wye.ac.uk/
Now linked with Imperial College, London, Wye College is known all over the world for its research-led teaching in biological sciences, the environment, agriculture and horticulture. It runs programmes of study on campus at first degree and postgraduate level, postgraduate programmes of study by distance learning, and short courses for continuing professional development.

Other Internet Handbooks to help you

Travel & Holidays on the Internet, Graham Jones (Internet Handbooks).

10 Famous gardens and gardeners

In this chapter we will explore:

▶ *famous gardens in the UK*
▶ *celebrity gardeners*
▶ *famous gardens in Europe*
▶ *famous gardens around the world*

In this chapter we will take a brief look at a number of famous gardens and gardeners. The gardens that we have covered are delightful, and if you have not been there, you can at least go on a virtual tour.

Famous gardens in the UK

One of the best ways to get ideas for your own garden is to visit other people's gardens, particularly some of the smaller and less well known gardens belonging to private individuals. These gardens can be a mine of inspiration and quite often the owner is available to talk to, which is not often the case with the larger gardens open to the public.

National Gardens Scheme
http://www.ngs.org.uk
The best way to find out about which gardens are open and when is to visit the web site of the National Gardens Scheme (figure 83). This is a charity that raises money by opening gardens to the public. The details and opening times are published annually in their famous Yellow Book. On the website you can search their database for information about the gardens that belong to the scheme. There is also a featured garden which you can visit and details of other events taking place throughout the year.

Fig. 83. The UK National Gardens Scheme raises money by opening gardens to the public.

119

Famous gardens and gardeners ....

Address http://www.barnsdalegardens.co.uk/

Tuesday, Ma

Barnsdale Gardens

Visiting Details ►
Book Your Visit ►
How To Find Us ►
The Gardens ►
Geoff Hamilton ►
News ►
Tips ►
In The Gardens ►
Competition ►
Links ►
Contact Details ►
Shopping ►
Barnsdale Raffle ►
Downloads ►

SEARCH

Click on map of gardens above or use link to the gardens on left.

The gardens at Barnsdale in Rutland were built by Britains best loved Television gardener Geoff Hamilton over several years for BBC TV Gardeners' World programme & various other BBC specials.

Fig. 84. Barnsdale Gardens in Rutland, created by the late Geoff Hamilton, the popular television presenter.

Barnsdale Gardens
http://www.barnsdalegardens.co.uk/
There can be few UK-based gardeners who have not heard of the late Geoff Hamilton. He was the gardener who came into our homes both as part of BBC's weekly Gardener's World and in other television series such as Paradise Gardens and The Cottage Garden. Geoff died in 1996, whilst raising money for charity. Since then, the gardens he created have been opened to the public. This is a delightful site, well worth a visit (figure 84).

Bodnant Gardens, North Wales
http://www.sissons.demon.co.uk/bodnant.htm
Sisley Tours takes you to the famous Bodnant Gardens in north Wales. Before writing this book, we visited the gardens and they are breathtaking. The gardens lie above the River Conwy on ground that slopes to the south west and looks across the valley towards the Snowdon range. The garden itself is in two parts. The upper part around the house consists of the Terrace Gardens and informal lawns shaded by trees. The lower part is called the Dell, formed by the valley of the Afon Hiraethlyn, a tributary of the Conwy. Bodnant also has National Collections of *rhododendron forrestii*, magnolia, eucryphia and embothrium. The gardens have wheelchairs, and braille guides for the visually impaired.

Borde Hill Garden
http://www.bordehill.co.uk
Borde Hill is a garden of contrasts that captures the imagination and delights the senses. It is set in 200 acres of a traditional country estate in the area of outstanding natural beauty lying between the town of Haywards Heath and the village of Cuckfield in mid Sussex. The garden and parkland were established at the turn of the century from the great plant

collectors who travelled to the Himalayas, China, Burma, Tasmania and the Andes. They contain the best private collection of champion trees in Britain and one of the most comprehensive collections of trees and shrubs in the world. The garden in Sussex has its own page with useful information and photographs from the garden. This informative site includes a location map, and links to other interesting sites.

Capability Brown
http://www.gardenvisit.com/b/brown1.htm
This is a useful site to explore the story of the famous eighteenth-century English landscape designer, Lancelot 'Capability' Brown, who worked at Blenheim, Chatsworth and many other famous locations.

Cornwall Calling
http://www.cornwall-calling.co.uk/gardens.htm
Opening with a handy clickable map, this site covers Heligan and several other houses and gardens in Cornwall such as Edgcumbe, Lanhydrock and Cotehele. Why not make it a long weekend? It is well worth visiting many of the gardens in this beautiful part of the country.

Exbury
http://www.exbury.co.uk/exbury.htm
The famous Exbury Gardens near Southampton are well known for the beautiful rhododendrons, camellias and azaleas that thrive there. The gardens were created by Lionel de Rothschild, a voracious collector of plants, particularly rhododendrons and azaleas. He was also a highly successful hybridiser of many different species and Exbury is still filled with his creations. This tradition has been continued by his descendants, his sons Edmund and Leopold, who continue to develop the gardens today (figure 85).

Fig. 85. The famous Exbury gardens created by the Rothschild family, near Lyndhurst in the New Forest in Hampshire.

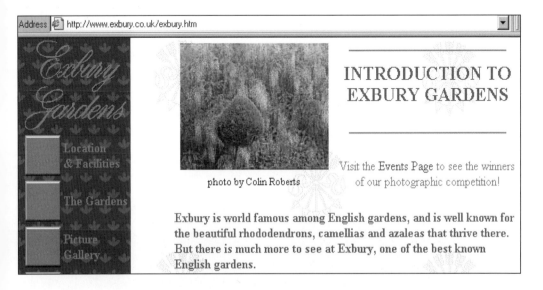

Address | http://www.exbury.co.uk/exbury.htm

Exbury Gardens

Location & Facilities

The Gardens

Picture Gallery

INTRODUCTION TO EXBURY GARDENS

photo by Colin Roberts

Visit the Events Page to see the winners of our photographic competition!

Exbury is world famous among English gardens, and is well known for the beautiful rhododendrons, camellias and azaleas that thrive there. But there is much more to see at Exbury, one of the best known English gardens.

Famous gardens and gardeners ....

Graham's Paradise Garden
http://www.maigold.co.uk
Another delightful garden, but on a much smaller scale, is Graham's Paradise Garden. This tiny garden is situated near Manchester and is crammed full of interesting things to see. The web site is a delight with hundreds of colourful photographs and a lot of information on different groups of plants – roses, clematis, camellias, daphnes, delphiniums, geraniums, hellebores, roses, penstemons and more. You'll also discover a winter garden, and a delightful pond as well as information about the visiting wildlife. The pages are regularly updated and you can chat to other gardeners or ask gardening questions. You can visit this garden for real between February and September, by appointment. The money raised is given to charity.

The Eden Project
http://www.edenproject.com/welcome.html
This is the new under-glass project being established in an old china clay pit, in Cornwall. The project describes itself as a living theatre telling the story of plants and people. This is an excellent site for gardeners, scientists and anyone with an interest in the environment. It is a must for both a virtual visit and a trip to Cornwall.

Heligan: The Lost Gardens
http://www.cornwall-calling.co.uk/homes-and-gardens/heligan.htm
These gardens are a delight and well worth a trip to Mevagissey in Cornwall. There are some delightful photographs of the gardens on this site (figure 86). They consist of pleasure grounds, walled gardens, and a huge vegetable garden. The house was built in 1603 by William Tremayne. The estate was self-sufficient with its own quarries, woods, farms, brick works, flourmill, sawmill, brewery, and productive orchards and gardens. The gardens were created mainly in the 19th century, with 57 acres of planted gardens, about 100 acres of ornamental woodlands, and 300 acres of rides.

Fig. 86. The Lost Gardens of Heligan.

122

Heligan (Sisley Garden Tours)
http://www.sissons.demon.co.uk/heligan.htm
Here is another Heligan web site that is worth a look, illustrated with photographs.

Heligan (Tarbert Hotel)
http://www.tarbert-hotel.co.uk/heligan.htm
This page about Heligan is produced by the Tarbert Hotel in Penzance, Cornwall.

Heligan: The Official Site
http://www.heligan.com/home/home.html
This is the official Heligan site, which with its sepia illustrations seems rather tame compared with others. The site also takes a little while to download. There are links to a garden tour, a Heligan shop, education, head gardener, a great gardens offer, special events, friends of Heligan, and other links.

Hestercombe House
http://www.sisley.co.uk/hstrcmbe.htm
Hestercombe House stands near the village of Cheddon Fitzpaine, close to Taunton on the south-facing slopes of the Quantock Hills. It was originally the home of gentleman farmer Coplestone Warre-Bampfylde. He inherited the estate in 1750 and began to develop a garden. Amazingly this garden was lost beneath thousands of tons of silt. A woodland overgrew it, until in 1991 local man Philip White found that a classic garden landscape had existed in the valley behind the house, and began to restore the gardens. The gardens are open to the public and you can see the work ongoing. This web address is part of a web site run by Sisley Tours. It contains details of Hestercombe and how you can visit.

Sir Harold Hillier Gardens and Arboretum
http://www.hillier.hants.gov.uk/
This is a diverse collection of hardy trees and shrubs from around the world, started by the late Sir Harold Hillier in 1953 and now covering 180 acres. Within this unique collection of some 42,000 plants (12,000 different types), there is something of interest for everyone throughout the year. To discover whether a particular plant or group of plants is represented in the collection, you can search the online plant records database at this web site. The information available includes the locations for most plants within the Gardens. You are also invited to email them at hillier@-hants.gov.uk with your botanical and horticultural queries.

Kew Gardens (Royal Botanic Garden)
http://www.kew.org.uk
The Kew Gardens web site is called Kew Web (figure 87). A map guides you around the world-famous gardens, and gives you information and pictures of the main plant collections and other features, plus a seasonal guide to what is flowering when. The site tells you about the many famous people have contributed their skills and expertise to the success

Famous gardens and gardeners ....

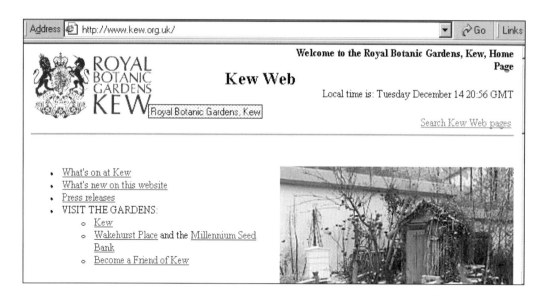

Fig. 87. Kew Web is the name of the web site of the Royal Botanic Gardens at Kew, outside London.

of the Royal Botanic Gardens across the centuries – architects, botanical illustrators, botanists, gardeners, curators, designers, directors, horticultural advisers, patrons and benefactors. Kew Web is also a good source for botanical and scientific information such as poisonous fungi. There are links to information on plant species, and Kew Web also provides good links with many other botanical sites in UK and around the world. The site has recently been relaunched. Over the next few months they will be adding more images and information on their science and horticulture activities.

Margery Fish Gardens, East Lambrook Manor
http://www.margeryfish.com
Through her many books and articles Margery Fish became, after Vita Sackville-West, one of the most admired gardeners and garden writers of her day, developing the concept of a 'cottage garden'. Her passion for nature and her skill in mixing plants in a contained space, yet in different environments, made her ideas relevant to all gardeners.

National Botanic Garden of Wales
http://www.gardenofwales.org.uk
The National Botanic Garden of Wales at Llanarthne in Carmarthenshire is dedicated to science, education and leisure, with the broad study of plants and sustainable solutions at its heart. The 568-acre Middleton Hall estate of William Paxton has provided walled gardens, lakes and cascades for restoration. The formal gardens with their centrepiece building, The Great Glasshouse, designed by Norman Foster, takes up about a third of this area. The rest of the land is made up of species-rich grassland and woodland that is being converted to a demonstration organic farm. Among the features of the web site are an aquatic ecology laboratory, a genetic garden, a 'bioverse', and a science centre.

Ness Botanical Gardens
http://www.merseyworld.com/nessgardens/
When the Liverpool cotton merchant Arthur Kilpin Bulley began to create a garden in 1898, part of which he opened to local residents, he laid the foundations of one of the major botanic gardens in the UK. Today they are owned and managed by Liverpool University. The web site includes details of a year-round programme of lectures on such topics as testing new plants for the garden from bedding plants to trees, activities in British Gardens over the past century, and exotic botany.

Phoenix Park, Dublin
http://www.iol.ie/resource/imi/rehab/
This is a wonderful idea. As environmental protection moves up the political ladder, you can do your bit – at least, you can if you have Irish lineage. Take a look at the site, and see how you can sponsor Irish tree regeneration. It appears to be pitched at an American audience.

Real Gardens
http://www.channel4.com/
Monty Don's Channel Four programme is shown on this site, which represents it well (figure 88). Monty is a gardener himself and writes for a number of national dailies on gardening. An online resources section includes garden design, alpine gardens, herbs, annuals and perennials, fruit and vegetables, bulbs, and organic gardening.

Fig. 88. Real Gardens, a useful information resource.

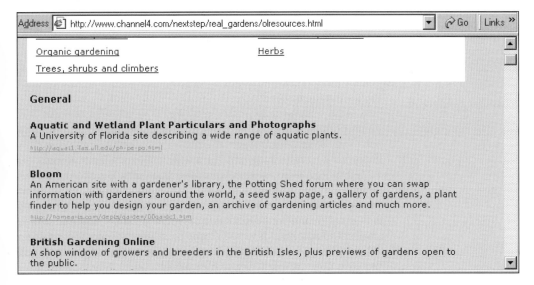

Royal Botanic Garden Edinburgh
http://www.rbge.org.uk
The rather academic-looking site gives substantial information about the background and work of the Royal Botanic Garden, including education, research, and publications. It includes a searchable version of the Flora Europaea database.

Famous gardens and gardeners ....

Royal Parks
http://www.open.gov.uk/rp/rphome.htm
London's Royal Parks include Hyde Park, Kensington Gardens, St James's Park and The Green Park, Regent's Park and Primrose Hill, Greenwich Park, Richmond Park and Bushy Park. The Royal Parks Agency aims to manage them so that they offer peaceful enjoyment, recreation, entertainment and delight to all. The Agency also manages Brompton Cemetery and a number of other open spaces, including Parliament Square and Victoria Tower Gardens. The web site home page contains a clickable scaled map which shows all the garden locations.

Sissinghurst Castle (Tour)
http://www.tka.co.uk/sisley/sisnghst.htm
Nearer to home are the famous gardens at Sissinghurst Castle in Kent. This Sisley Garden Tours site links well to details about Vita Sackville-West, the garden designer. She and her husband Harold Nicolson bought the badly damaged castle in 1930 and began the major work of restoring both the house and the garden. The result is a magnificent garden.

Sissinghurst: Enjoy Britain
http://www.enjoybritain.co.uk/counties/Kent/Sissinghurst135ise.cfm
This web site offers a visual tour of Sissinghurst through photographs (if you can find them).

Sissinghurst
http://www.woodhamhall.demon.co.uk/surround/siss.cast.html
More details of Sissinghurst can be found here, but this time it is practicalities such as opening times.

Stowe Landscape Garden
http://www.stowe.co.uk
Among large gardens, the Stowe School web site captured our imagination. The Stowe Landscape Garden in Buckinghamshire is a very important and historic garden associated with such famous designers as Vanbrugh, William Kent and Lancelot 'Capability' Brown. The garden is famous for many reasons. Its very size is impressive: 250 acres within the garden alone, enclosed by nearly two miles of ha-ha (a dry ditch lined with a wall on the garden side so that neither ditch nor wall was usually visible). Outside extends a much larger park. The site takes you on a tour of the garden, with the aid of a clickable map, and even allows you to view Stowe in 360° with its Quicktime VR (virtual reality) movies.

University of Durham Botanic Garden
http://www.dur.ac.uk/~deb0www/dubg/bghomep.html
The pages were undergoing a major re-design when reviewed.

Wakehurst Place
http://www.rbgkew.org.uk/wakehurst/index.html
This is Kew Gardens' sister garden, near Ardingly in West Sussex. The

environmental conditions of the High Weald of Sussex contrast with those of Kew by offering varied topography, higher rainfall and more diverse and moisture retentive soils. A range of microclimates enable the successful cultivation of a great diversity of plants, many of which do not thrive at Kew. The site includes visitor information, garden features, the living collections, seasonal interest, and the Millennium Seedbank project.

Wisley (Royal Horticultural Society)
http://www.rhs.org.uk
No mention of famous gardens to visit would be complete without mentioning Wisley. The RHS home page gives direct links to their gardens. Probably the best-known one is Wisley. It is set in 240 acres and offers much for the virtual or real gardener. Penelope Hobhouse has a country garden at Wisley. This is a plantsman's garden with formal rectilinear pathways and terracing. There is also a temperate glasshouse and a 'garden of the senses'. There is also a link to the garden at Hyde Hall in Essex, donated to the RHS in 1993 and containing the national collection of malus and viburnum. There is also link to the gardens at Rosemoor in Devon.

Celebrity gardeners

All Things British – British Bookshop
http://www.allthingsbritish.com/bookshop/gardens/enggaring.html
This site is a bookshop which contains gardening titles by famous authors, too many to mention here. There are clickable subject categories ranging from organic vegetables to medicinal gardening. There is also a free newsletter.

Charlie Dimmock ScreenSaver
http://www.gardenersworld.beeb.com/gw/tvrm/199910.charlie.tips/
page01/
We cannot guarantee that it will be there when you log on, but at the time of writing the *Gardeners World* web site had a free screensaver download of Charlie Dimmock, with some stunning photographs.

Ground Force (BBC)
http://www.bbc.co.uk/groundforce/bio.shtml
This is the official web site *of Ground Force*, the popular BBC2 television programme broadcast on Friday evenings. Here you will find profiles of Alan Titchmarsh, Charlie Dimmock, Tommy Walsh and Will Shanahan. These pages are based within the main BBC site, and are complete with a web guide and gardening tips (figure 89). You can join in the online chat on the Home & Garden message board.

Ground Force Fan Site
http://www.ground-force.co.uk
This is a delightful fan site for the hit TV series of the same name, maintained by Susan Warwick. There is a lot of detail about the programme's presenters, anchorman Alan Titchmarsh, water garden expert, Charlie

Famous gardens and gardeners ....

Fig. 89. The official web site for Ground Force, the popular BBC Television gardening series presented by Alan Titchmarsh, Charlie Dimmock and Tommy Walsh.

Dimmock, and of course Tommy 'Two days' Walsh. The site has been very helpful for gardeners wanting to keep up to date with the show.

Gardens: Europe

Arboretum National des Barre (France)
http://www.coeur-de-france.com/arboretum-des-barres.html
The page is in French, and has a link to ENGREF (Ecole Nationale du Génie Rural des Eaux et des Forêts).

Garden Web Europe
http://www.uk.gardenweb.com/
Among the many gardening resources available on this useful web site is a searchable directory of gardens in Europe. On the home page click on Directory (Gardens). There are hyperlinks to the web pages of the gardens mentioned.

Giverny (France)
http://www.mmfa.qc.ca/visite-vr/anglais/index.html
Another on our list of must-visit gardens are Claude Monet's beautiful gardens at Giverny, the inspiration for his famous water lilies paintings. The page offers a virtual tour of the garden (figure 90). You use your mouse to guide a little figure through the garden and discover works by the impressionist master as you go. The web site was published to mark the Montreal exhibition of 1999.

Giverny (France)
http://www.giverny.org/gardens/index.htm
There are many more Monet-related sites than we can list here, but this one is certainly the most impressive. It is in both French and English. It gives lots of background about the house and gardens. 'The rectangular Clos Normand, with archways of climbing plants entwined around bril-

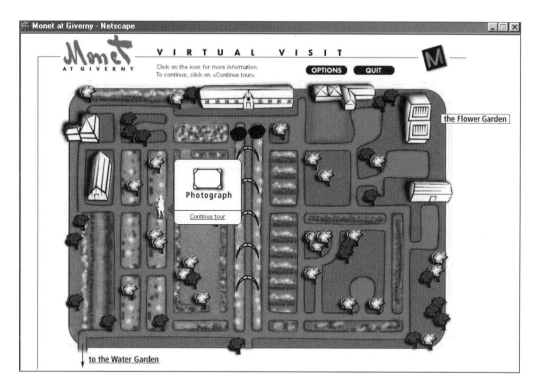

Fig. 90. Monet's garden at
Giverney. This web site
lets you take a virtual tour
of the garden, using your
mouse.

liantly coloured shrubs, lies before the house and studios, offering from
spring to autumn the palette of varying colours of the painter-gardener
who was 'ecstatic about flowers'. Lastly, the Water Garden, formed by a
tributary of the Epte, lies further away, shaded by weeping willows. With
its famous Japanese Bridge, its wistarias, azaleas and its pond, it has
once more become that casket of sky and water which inspired the pic-
torial universe of the water lilies.'

Guatiza, Lanzarote – Cactus Garden (Spain)
http://www.lanzarote.com/LugJardinCactus-in.html
Lanzarote is more than just a package holiday location. You can explore
some delightful aspects of the island, one of which is the cactus garden.
One of the key people on the island was the late artist, Cesar Manrique. A
man of vision, he became a politician and stopped high-rise building on
the island. The garden itself is gorgeous, the hot climate being conducive
to some unusual cacti. The cacti farms nearby are an impressive sight. The
cacti are homes for cochinillas, small parasites that live on the cacti. When
they are dead, dried and ground into a paste, they form the extraordinary
dye called cochinille – cochineal – used in cosmetics and dyes for its
qualities and resistance to external agents.

Palmengarten, Frankfurt (Germany)
http://www.stadt-frankfurt.de/palmengarten
The Palmengarten was established as a trust in Frankfurt in 1868. It is a
botanical park which displays flowers and other flora throughout the

year. Its 50 acres also offer a wide variety of recreation. The Palmengarten is known worldwide for its collection of tropical plants. The photographs on this quick-loading site are of unusually high quality. The site has some pages in English.

Tivoli Gardens, Copenhagen (Denmark)
http://www.tivoligardens.com/
The famous Tivoli Gardens in central Copenhagen opened in 1843. An architect named Carstensen persuaded the Danish king to lease him a site for a park modelled on the now-defunct Parisian Tivoli and London's Vauxhall Gardens. The Tivoli includes rides and entertainments as well as the famous gardens. Under its charter, 75 per cent of the site has to be open space, and that rule – still observed – is why Tivoli still feels more like a public garden than a theme park.

Versailles (France)
http://www.chateauversailles.fr
There are some spectacular sights at Versailles, just outside Paris, including some of the most stunning water features to be found anywhere in the world. Originally the grounds were eight times bigger than they are today, and what is now Le Grand Parc was once the lesser park. The ditches were originally designed as 'wolf plunges' to prevent wolves from entering. The site then goes on to say: 'The grounds are organised around the Grand Canal, an ornamental body of water covering 44 hectares (105 acres) and measuring seven kilometres (over four miles) around its edges. The main axis extends the vista infinitely westward between a rank of tall Italian poplars whose proud silhouettes can just be seen beyond the water. At the head of the canal, buildings called Little Venice evoke gondoliers with their gondolas, yachts and galleys, comprising a whole fleet used for outings, concerts, and nautical festivities. The perpendicular branch of the canal, meanwhile, linked the Menagerie (no longer extant) to the Trianon.' This is an appealing site, and if you are visiting France, well worth checking out.

Versailles (France)
http://members.dynasty.net/jmoats/versailles/index.htm
This is another brilliantly constructed site, which is bilingual in French and English, so you can practise your français.

Gardens: rest of the world

American Association of Botanic Gardens and Arboreta (USA)
http://www.aabga.org/
Founded in 1940, the AABGA is the professional association for public gardens in North America. It supports the public horticulture community in its mission to study, display, and conserve plants. The web site contains some useful links to its member gardens throughout the USA. Institutional membership has grown from 100 to 490 and individual membership from 800 to almost 3,000.

Arnold Arboretum, Harvard University (USA)
http://arboretum.harvard.edu
The Arnold Arboretum is a research and educational institution. The web site presents its collection of hardy trees, shrubs and vines located on 265 acres in Boston, Massachusetts, and associated herbarium and library collections.

Australian National Botanic Gardens
http://155.187.10.12/anbgjervis-bay.html
The ANBG maintains a scientific collection of native plants from all parts of Australia. These are displayed for the enjoyment and education of visitors, and used for research into classification and biology. A herbarium of preserved plant specimens is closely associated with the living collection. The ANBG also cultivates plants threatened in the wild. The site includes links to other botanic gardens in Australia.

Mamiku Gardens (West Indies)
http://www.mamiku.com
For something exotic, explore the web site of Mamiku Gardens, the finest botanical gardens in St Lucia. You can take a virtual tour of the gardens, which include 12 acres of landscaped gardens and woodlands, an archaeological site under excavation, a creole bush medicine garden, and endangered St Lucian trees.

New York Botanical Garden (USA)
http://www.nybg.org
One of the oldest and largest botanical gardens in the world, the NYBG in the Bronx is a museum of plants and a national historic landmark. There are 250 acres of grounds, and 47 gardens and plant collections featuring day lilies, herbs, native plants, perennials, alpines, roses, annuals, magnolias, and tulips, as well as thousands of shrubs and trees.

Appendix: How to get on the net

In this chapter we will explore:

▶ *what is the internet?*

▶ *how do I get started?*

▶ *choosing an internet service provider (ISP)*

▶ *going online*

▶ *when your computer crashes*

▶ *finding out more*

It may seem perverse to place this section at the back of the book, but many people are already using the internet and do not need advice on how to get started. If you are new to the net, however, this section offers a helping hand.

What is the internet ?

Put at its simplest, the internet is a vast global network of computers, linked together by the world's telephone systems. By linking up, you too will become part of the internet. You can access vast amounts of information by connecting in a few seconds to millions of other computers on the network.

There is a common idea that, to be on the internet, you need to be a bit of a geek or a nerd – a computer boffin. Not so. Life today means that most people will have access to computers, just as most have access to a telephone or television set. We are increasingly living what some experts call a 'web lifestyle'.

The internet comprises several elements. The main ones in rough order of popularity are:

1. email
2. the world wide web – 'the web', millions of web sites and web pages
3. Usenet – a network of some 80,000 newsgroups and millions of messages a day
4. chat – chat channels and chat rooms, especially Internet Relay Chat (IRC)
5. WAP – wireless application protocol, enabling the use of mobile phones on the internet
6. Other technologies such as FTP (file transfer protocol), telnet and gopher.

Some of these technologies now cross over with one another (e.g. web-based chat or web-based newsgroups), so that the terms 'internet' and 'web' are becoming interchangeable.

How do I get started?

Basically, you need four things: a computer, a telephone line, a modem, and an internet service provider.

Your computer
There are main two types of computer, the personal computer ('PC'), and the Apple Macintosh ('Mac'). Both will get you on the net, though PCs predominate. Each type has its pros and cons. If you are looking at buying a computer, shop around. Make sure that you are happy with what you are getting, before you part with your cash. Make a careful note of the specifications, and prices. You could even find someone locally to assemble one to your own specification, which could well work out cheaper than buying a machine off the shelf.
Your computer equipment should comprise:

1. a fast Pentium III-type processor (typically 200 to 700 megahertz or 'clock speed')
2. memory (typically 32 to 128 megabytes of RAM – random access memory)
3. a hard disk drive (typical capacity of between 1 and 10 gigabytes) – called the 'C' drive
4. a floppy disk drive – called the 'A' drive
5. a CD rom drive – usually designated as the 'D' drive
6. an operating system (OS) such as Microsoft Windows 98
7. a monitor (typically with a 15 to 19 inch screen)
8. an internal or external modem
9. a sound card
10. a video/graphics card
11. a pair of speakers
12. a keyboard
13 a mouse

Desirable extras:
14. a printer
15. a scanner
16 a digital camera
17. a bundle of free but useful software (e.g. a word processor, spread-sheet package, anti-virus software)

In computers, you pretty much get what you pay for. Whatever your final choice, modern computers represent fantastic value in terms of what they can do. Get the most powerful specification you can reasonably afford. Average systems cost between £500 and £1,000.

What is a modem?
For internet access, you will need a modem attached to your computer. A

modem is a small gadget that connects your computer to the telephone system. There are two types of modem: an internal one (fitted inside your computer), and an external one (which you plug into the back of the computer, and which costs between around £40 and £80.

There is now an industry standard for modems: V90. If you are tempted to buy a secondhand one, make sure it is a V90. Your modem should also be at least 56k. The 56 indicates the speed that it will access the internet. The faster the modem, faster your internet experience will be.

Choosing an internet service provider (ISP)

You need to sign up with an internet service provider. This is a company that will link you to the global internet. In the UK there are several hundred ISPs to choose from – and over 10,000 worldwide. The most widely used in the UK include Freeserve (associated with Dixons and PC World), America OnLine (AOL), Compuserve, BT Internet, Virgin Net and Demon Internet. Ask the advice of your friends who are online, or ask the shop where you bought your PC.

Important considerations

▶ *Local calls* – Make sure that your internet calls are local calls. Your internet service provider (ISP) should have a local presence. Your computer then dials up their local computer, which connects you to the internet. So once you are on the internet you only pay local call rates, even if you are viewing web pages, or emailing someone, halfway across the world.

▶ *Support* – The second consideration is the ISP support facilities. There will be times when, despite your best efforts, your computer will refuse to work. We originally used an ISP some distance away. We experienced a day of hell when our computer would not work; seven hours of long-distance calls failed to solve the problem. We then changed to a new company which offered local 24-hour support. Some ISPs charge a small monthly fee in return for unlimited online support. If you do not pay this, it will typically cost you 50p to £1 per minute to speak to their helpline. Our mega crash could have bankrupted us – seven hours on the telephone at £1 per minute!

Loading the CD rom
When you have chosen an ISP, they should give you a free CD rom to fire up your machine. Simply pop it into the CD drive, and after a few seconds delay it should start to load automatically. It will display a series of screens which step you through the installation and sign-up process. You should be ready to go onto the internet within four or five minutes.

Among the various items of software loaded by the CD rom will be a browser. This is an essential software programme for using the internet. It enables you to view web pages, send and receive email, and help you manage your internet experience in all kinds of ways. Your browser will typically be one of these:

1. Microsoft Internet Explorer (which includes Outlook Express for sending and receiving email, and accessing newsgroups)
2. Netscape Navigator or Netscape Communicator (which includes Netscape Messenger for sending and receiving email, and accessing newsgroups)

Many people use America Online as their internet service provider. AOL is unique in providing its own proprietary browser. Like the other two browsers, it enables you to send and receive email, access newsgroups, and manage your internet experience. Other possible browsers include NetCaptor and Opera.

Going online

Logging on for the first time
On a PC, click Start, then Programs, look for the name of your ISP and click on it. Your computer should then automatically dial up to your ISP. (Alternatively, a new icon may have appeared on your desktop, created by your ISP as part of the installation process. You can click on that instead.)

You will normally have to enter your user name and password. Your browser will open up, and display your 'home page' – probably the home page of your ISP. You don't have to stick with this, though it may be useful until you find your way around. You can decide to have a different start-up page later, if you wish, by altering the settings in your browser.

This page will be full of links you can click on to get you started with your internet experience. For example, there will be a search facility – a button or a little text box – which enables you to search for anything you want on the internet. For guidance on searching, refer to Chapter 1 of this book, or to the book *Where to Find It on the Internet* published in the Internet Handbooks series.

Do I have to tell anyone when I am online?
No, you can go online whenever you want. BT or your telephone company will charge you the cost of the calls you make to your internet service provider, normally at local phone rates.

What about free internet access?
There is an increasing trend towards completely free access to the internet, i.e. free of all telephone call charges. To find the very latest information, use a search engine such as Yahoo! or AltaVista, and do a keyword search. For example, you could key in the words 'free internet access'. Remember, you are free to change your ISP at any time, or install an extra one.

Should I disable call waiting?
You will have to disable 'call waiting', if you have it. This is the device

where the phone bleeps to tell you another caller is waiting to reach you. Type in #43# on the keypad of your phone. This will disable the call waiting facility. This means that when you are on the internet ('surfing the net'), the call waiting will not work, so your local call to the internet cannot be interrupted. If you leave call waiting on, the bleeps will intercept your local internet call and cut you off. You will then have to reconnect yourself to the internet.

How do I start call waiting again, after I have finished on the internet?
Just key in *43# on the keypad of your phone. This will restart your call waiting facility so that you can use the phone just as before.

When is the best time of day to use the internet?
Your connection in the UK should be no more than the cost of a local call. Do check with your ISP to make sure about this. Since local calls are cheaper in the evening and at weekends, this means it is cheaper to surf the internet at these times.

Remember, the internet is a global network, and still dominated by the United States. The UK is roughly 5 to 8 hours ahead of the USA. This means that until around 2pm GMT it is quite easy to get onto the internet and find what you want. But 2pm GMT is 9am in many parts of the USA, the time when millions of people are going to work and logging onto the internet. Internet traffic is thereby increased and internet communications slow down. In the USA local calls are free (though standing charges may be higher than in the UK). So when America goes to work in the morning, internet usage soars. When web sites are being accessed by a lot of people at the same time, pages can be noticeably slower to download.

When your computer crashes

Sooner or later, everyone has a partial or complete computer crash. It can seem alarming the first time it happens. Whatever key you press, or however much you click your mouse, little or nothing seems to happen. Stay calm. On your keyboard, try pressing Ctrl + Alt + Delete, all at the same time. This might shut down the program which is causing a problem. If that doesn't work, pressing the same keys again should restart your computer. If you cannot even do this, just switch off the computer, wait for 10 to 15 seconds, then switch it on again (a 'cold reboot'). If the crash happened when you were in the middle of working on something, your computer may run an automatic system check called Scandisk. This could take two or three minutes, correcting any problems, following which your Desktop should reappear. However, any of your unsaved work may well be lost.

System Mechanic
http://www.Iolo.com
Whilst writing this book we had a computer crash, and our Windows Registry (which stores important information on the computer) was damaged. We saw a review in a well-known UK computer magazine for a download from this web site. The software is called System Mechanic. It sits on the desktop and quietly keeps your PC working at its optimum.

You can try it free for 30 days, and the support service is excellent. Highly recommended.

Viruses

Viruses are a relatively rare but growing threat to everyone who uses a computer for accessing the internet, or for sharing disks with other people. Viruses may be transmitted maliciously, or by accident. Once they install themselves on your computer, they can destroy many other files, use your address book to copy themselves to all your friends, and even wipe your entire hard disk. The end result is a lot of grief, expense, destruction of data, and wasted time. A good discipline is to back up all your own files regularly, onto some external medium such as a floppy diskette, zip disk or rewritable CD rom.

Viruses are of two main types:

1. Viruses in program files – these files could be any kind of software, from games software to business packages, or utility programs of various kinds. It is wise not to download any program file from the internet without first running a virus check over it.

2. Viruses hidden in Word files, which may arrive by email. Resist the (possibly strong) temptation to open any email from any sender you do not recognise. Just delete such emails. They are probably junk mail ('spam') in any case. Definitely avoid opening any files attached to such emails.

The well-known anti-virus software packages include McAfee, Dr Solomon's, and Norton/Symantec. Such packages are available online, or from any good computer store for something like £40 to £60. It is essential to have up-to-date versions, since new viruses appear all the time.

Visit the free Internet HelpZone at
www.internet-handbooks.co.uk
Helping you master the internet

Further reading and reference

This section deals with:

▶ *online gardening dictionaries and encyclopedias*
▶ *online bookshops*
▶ *Internet Handbooks*

Online gardening dictionaries and encyclopedias

This section offers a selection of useful gardening reference guides available to you on the internet. Don't be stuck for a botanical or horticultural definition again!

Botany Encyclopedia of Plants and Botanical Dictionary
http://www.botany.com/
This reference resource covers all kinds of annuals, bulbs, cactus, succulents, fruit, grasses, water plants, herbs, spices, houseplants, perennials, shrubs, bushes, trees, vegetables, vines and wild flowers.

Botany Zone
http://www.botanyzone.com/
This is a searchable plant database covering general gardening techniques and herbal qualities. There is information about growing plants, gardening, the nutritional, herbal and medicinal values of plants, landscaping ideas, resources for exotic and native plants, and a vast amount more.

Fig. 91. The Garden Web Glossary of Botanical Terms, an excellent example of the kind of reference freely available over the internet today.

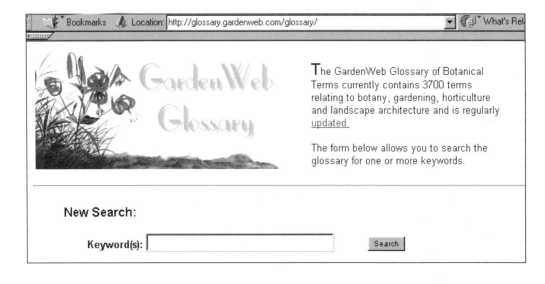

Directory of Herbs
http://garden.cas.psu.edu/vegcrops/herbs.html
This resource has been compiled by the Department of Horticulture, the Pennsylvania State University – everything from anise and apple mint to thyme and yarrow.

Garden Web Glossary of Botanical Terms
http://www.gardenweb.com/glossary/
Garden Web (figure 91) has developed this useful interactive glossary of 3,700 terms relating to botany, gardening, horticulture and landscape architecture. If you are looking up names of plants, there is a separate plant database here. The information is continually updated.

Horticultural Dictionary
http://www.agnic.org/agdb/hortdict.html
This is a dictionary of over 15,000 gardening related terms presents the user with a simple search interface. The users enters a search string' and the system returns all known references. AgDB, in the web address above, is part of the Agriculture Network Information Centre. It is a database directory of agriculture-related databases, datasets, and information systems. It describes and links to more than 1,100 information resources around the world.

New Royal Horticultural Society Dictionary of Gardening
http://www.grovereference.com/Science/RHSDictionary.htm
This famous published work covers over 60,000 plants, complemented by over 4,000 botanical line drawings, to create the most comprehensive reference work on gardening and horticulture available. It is available in printed form, not (yet) as an online database.

Online bookshops

Alphabetstreet Books
http://www.alphabetstreet.com
This is one of the leading UK online bookstores, started in 1996 and now backed by FreeServe. If you wish, free 'informers' – sent to you by email every two weeks or so – will keep you up to date on hundreds of subjects. You can search and browse for any book, and order using their secure internet credit and debit card payment system.

Amazon
http://www.amazon.com
Amazon.com opened its virtual doors in 1995 with a mission to transform book-buying into the fastest, easiest, and most enjoyable shopping experience possible. It has since achieved immortality (and a vast stockmarket value) in becoming the world's most popular online bookshop, with heavily discounted prices throughout. 12 million people in more than 160 countries have used it – not just for books but for electronic greeting cards, online auctions, CDs, videos, DVDs, toys and games, and electronics.

Further reading and reference ....

Amazon UK
http://www.amazon.co.uk
This is the UK version of Amazon, which is now developing localised versions for other countries. Payment for book purchases is by credit card. You become an account-holder, following which you can view your order history, review any of your past or pending orders, and track the progress of your order online. Amazon works with UK wholesalers, and so your book will normally arrive within a couple of days. You can easily change your email address or password at any time.

Blackwells
http://bookshop.blackwell.co.uk/
The 'world's leading academic bookseller' would like you to be not just a customer but a member. Registration is free, and brings the following benefits: an alerting service for new books listings by email, a one-time entry of up to four delivery addresses, a personalised notebook with access to your own events diary, order history and profile, and a personalised homepage. But it's not essential for using the site.

BOL
http://www.bol.com
BOL is a heavyweight contender in the online bookselling market, offering dedicated services for the UK, USA, Germany, France, the Netherlands, Spain and Switzerland. You can choose to create your own profile, tailoring the service to suit your individual requirements. You will then receive personalised book recommendations, details of new titles by your favourite authors and in your favourite subjects. You can also receive a personalised email newsletter with all the latest news about the books and authors you like best. You can easily check the status of your order. BOL (Bertelsmann Online) is a division of the media giant Bertlesmann.

Internet Bookshop (WH Smith Online)
http://www.bookshop.co.uk/
Originally an independent internet start up business, the Internet Bookshop has been rebranded as WHSmith Online. This attractive site offers well over a million titles in all subject areas, many of them discounted, and is very well presented in a magazine style format, with news, reviews and features. The sjte also sells CDs, videos and games. It uses a secure credit card ordering system.

Waterstones
http://www.waterstones.co.uk/
With its attractive presentation, quick search, links to branches, personal library, music, and numerous other features, Waterstones has developed an impressive and functional site. You can take a site tour, explore current title and author promotions, books of the month, signed first editions, out of print titles, and check out discounts on best-selling titles. You can check the status of your online order using a case-sensitive username and password. Recommended.

A table of gardening web sites

Acs	http://www.acs.edu.au/hort
Adao	http://www.adao.com/products/mainpr16.html
Agenet	http://www.agenet.com/ergo.garden.tools.html
Algardening	http://www.neosoft.com/internet/paml/groups.A/a1gardening.html
All Things British (bookshop)	http://www.allthingsbritish.com/bookshop/gardens/enggaring.html
Alpine Society	http://www.alpinegardensoc.demon.co.uk
AltaVista	http://www.altavista.com
American Hometime	http://www.pbs.org/hometime/
American Iris Society	http://www.irises.org/html
Aquamiser	http://www.garden-watering.com.
Aquatic Plants (email address)	majordomo@actwin.com
Ashfield College Dublin	http://www.ashfield-college.com/adult/gardening.htm
Ask Jeeves	http://www. askjeeves.com
Back Yard Nature	http://www.backyardnature.com/exec/gt/new.online.courses.html
Backyard Gardener	http://backyardgardener.com
Barnel	http://www.barnel.com/folding.html
Barnsdale Gardens	http://www.barnsdalegardens.co.uk/
Barnsley House	http://www.cotswolds-calling.com/houses-gardens/barnsley.htm
Bat Conservation Trust	http://www.bats.org.uk
Battle of the Flowers (Jersey)	http://www.battleoftheflowers.com
BBC Gardener's World Live	http://www.gardenersworld.beeb.com
BEGS (British & European Geranium Society)	http://www.fitzjohn.linkuk.co.uk
Berkshire College	http://www.berks-coll-ag.ac.uk/cpart.htm
Best Buys	http://bestbuysonthenet.com/bestbuys/gifts/312.htm
Bigfoot	http://www.bigfoot.co.uk
BIOSPH-L	listserv@listserv.aol.com
BK2Basics	listserv@drcoffsite.com
Bodnant Gardens, North Wales	http://www.sissons.demon.co.uk/bodnant.htm
Botany listservs	http://www.helsinki.fi/kmus/botnews.html
British Pelargonium & Geranium Society	http://www.homeusers.prestel.co.uk/1000feet/bps/.html
Canadian Gardening Online Garden Tours	http://canadiangardening.com/HTML/cg.gardentours.html
Canna Lily	http://www.farnborough.u-net.com/canna
Capability Brown	http://www.gardenvisit.com/b/brown1.htm
CataList Reference Site:	http://www.lsoft.com/lists/listref.html
Centre for Wholistic Living	http://ds.dial.pipex.com/town/estate/kaa46
Cesar Manrique	http://www.cesarmanrique.com/lbum%20de%20fotosi.htm
Charlie Dimmock Fan Club	http://www.geocities.com/TelevisionCity/Satellite/1311/index.html
Charlie Dimmock Fan Site	http://emporium.simplenet.com/charlie.htm
Charlie Dimmock Pond Feature	http://www.gardenersworld.beeb.com/gw/projects/pond
Charlie Dimmock Screensaver	http://www.gardenersworld.beeb.com/gw/tvrm/199910.charlie.tips/page01/
Chelsea Flower Show	http://ChelseaFlowerShow.htm
Clare Lusher	http://www.derby.org/clare/garden
Classic Kitchen Garden Design	http://www.bbg.org/gardening/kitchen/kitchen/simpson.html
Clematis	http://www.howells98.freeserve.co.uk
Compost	listproc@listproc.wsu.edu
Composter	http://www.composter.com/newsgroups.html
Cornwall Calling	http://www.cornwall-calling.co.uk/gardens.htm

A table of gardening web sites ....

Cyclamen Society	http://www.cyclamen.org
Delphinium Society	http://www.delphinium.demon.co.uk
Destination Europe	http://www.heartofeurope.com/itinchel.html
Dev-Habitat	dev-habitat-request@ihnet.it
Dig Magazine	http://www.digmagazine.com/96/9-96/sylvia.cfm
Dirt Doctor	http://www.dirtdoctor.com
Discovering Annuals	http://www.discoveringannuals.com
Dowdeswell Delphiniums	http://www.delphinium.co.nz
Ecolog-L	LISTSERV@umdd.umd.edu
English Gardening School	http://www.englishgardeningschool.co.uk
Ethology	LISTSERV@SEARN.sunet.se
Excite	http://www.excite.co.uk - http://www.excite.com
Expert Gardener	http://www.expertgardener.com
Flora Garden Tours	http://www.cam.net.uk/home/Flora.Garden.Tours/index.html
Frostproof	http://www.frostproof.com/catalog/hb-570.html
Garden Tours for Connoisseurs	http://www.aboutravel.com/spring02.html
Garden Tours.Com	http://www.gardentours.com/
Gardening UK	http://www.gardening-uk.co.uk/training.htm
Gardens	http://www.allseasons.demon.co.uk/gardens.htm
Gardens	listserv@ukcc.uky.edu
Gardens of Ireland	http://www.tourismresources.ie/cht/gardens.htm
Gardenscape	http://www.gardenscape.on.ca/pages/enablingtools.htm
Giverny (Monet's Garden)	http://www.arts.monash.edu.au/visarts/diva/giverny.html
Giverny (Monet's Garden)	http://www.giverny.org/monet/
Giverny (Monet's Garden)	http://www.mmfa.qc.ca/visite-vr/anglais/index.html
Graham's Paradise Garden	http://www.maigold.co.uk
Great Dixter tour	http://www.sissons.demon.co.uk/dixter.htm
Green Travel	majordomo@igc.apc.org
Ground Force (BBC Site)	http://www.bbc.co.uk/groundforce/bio.shtml
Ground Force (fan site)	http://freespace.virgin.net/susan.warwick/GF/main.htm
Groundwater	http://www.groundwater.com
Growing Potatoes (University of Idaho)	http://www.idbsu.edu/bsuradio/potato/growth.html
Hemerocallis	http://www.ofts.com/bill/daylily.html
Herb Advice	http://www.efn.org/–djz/birth/herbmain.html
Herb Society	http://www.herbsociety.co.uk
Herbs (Pennsylvania State University)	http://www.hortweb.cas.psu.edu/vegcrops/herbs.html
Hestercombe Gardens	www.hestercombe-gardens.co.uk
Hestercombe House South West Museums)	http://www.swmuseums.demon.co.uk/who.htm
Hestercombe House (Conference Facilities)	http://www.somerset.gov.uk/fire/fb.conf.htm
Hestercombe House (Sisley Tour)	http://www.sisley.co.uk/hstrcmbe.htm
Hidden Gardens of Ireland	http://www.gardentours.com/IrelandHiddenG.htm
Horticulture	listserv@vtvm1.cc.vt.edu
Hot Peppers	listserv@ucdmc.ucdavis.edu
Hotbot	http://www.hotbot.com
Hydra	http://www.hdra.org.uk/
Indiana Hand Center	http://www.indianahandcenter.com/easgardn.html
Infoseek	http://www.infoseek.co.uk - http://www.infoseek.com

Intec College	http://www.intec.edu.za/courses/create/gardhort.htm
International Water Lily & Water Garden Society	http://www.iwgs.org.
Irises	listserv@rt66.com
Japanese Garden Design Basics	http://www.camera.u-net.com/gardens/japanese/basics/basics.htm
Jo Anne Hillar	http://www.hillthablandscapes.co.za/great.htm
Kew Gardens	http://www.kew.org.uk
Kitchen Garden in Bloom (US magazine)	http://www.bbg.org/gardening/kitchen/kitchen/bales.html
Kitchen Gardener (US magazine)	http://www.finewoodworking.com/kg/admin/techniques.htm
Lanzarote	http://www.spaintour.com/lanza.htm
Le Jardin Secret	http://www.digicom.qc.ca/fleurdelotus/index.htm
List of Lists	http://catalog.com/vivian/interest-group-search.html
Liszt mailing lists	http://www.liszt.com
Looksmart	http://www.looksmart.com
Lost Gardens of Heligan	http://www.cornwall-calling.co.uk/homes-and-gardens/heligan.htm
Lost Gardens of Heligan (local hotel)	http://www.tarbert-hotel.co.uk/heligan.htm
Lost Gardens of Heligan (official site)	http://www.heligan.com/home/home.html
Lost Gardens of Heligan (Sisley tour)	http://www.sissons.demon.co.uk/heligan.htm
Lycos	http://www.lycos.co.uk - http://www.lycos.com
Master Gardening	listproc@listproc.wsu.edu
More on Barnsley House	http://virtual.clemson.edu/groups/hort/sctop/Englndtr/BrnslyHs/RVVegGdn.htm
More on Bodnant	http://www.oxalis.co.uk/bodnant.htm
National Gardening Scheme	http://www.ngs.org.uk
National Society for Allotment & Leisure Gardeners	http://www.nsalg.demon.co.uk/
Nature's World	http://www.nature'sworld.htm
Ness Gardens	http://www.merseyworld.com/nessgardens/
Organic gardening	listserv@lsv.uky.edu
Organic Gardening (USA magazine)	http://www.organicgardening.com
Osteospermums	http://www.gb-nl.freeserve.co.uk.
Oxford College of Design	http://www.ocgd.demon.co.uk
Peta	http://www.peta-uk.com/
Phoenix Park, Dublin	http://www.iol.ie/resource/imi/rehab/
Potager (French country style)	http://www.bbg.org/gardening/kitchen/kitchen/jones.html
Potatoes Online	http://www.spud.co.uk
Prairie Net	http://garden-gate.prairienet.org/maillist.htm
Publicly Accessible Mailing Lists	http://www.NeoSoft.com:80/internet/paml/bysubj.html
Quality of Perennials slide show	http://pss.uvm.edu/ppp/design/sld
Rakehandle	http://www.rakehandle.com/
Real Gardens	http://www.channel4.com/nextstep/real.gardens/olresources.html
Recovery Garden (Linda's Garden)	http://www.geocities.com/Heartland/Pointe/8391/recovery.html
Reference.Com (list database)	http://www.reference.com/
Regent Academy	http://www.regentacademy.com
Restoration Ecology (email address)	gadion@macc.wisc.edu
Roddy Llewellyn's Indoor Gardens	http://www.gsb.co.uk/breeze/homegarden/indoor-garden/home.html
Rosemary Verey's Barnsley House Tour	http://www.tka.co.uk/sisley/barnsley.htm
RotWeb	http://net.indra.co/~topsoil/compost.

A table of gardening web sites ....

Royal Horticultural Society	http://www.rhs.org.uk
Royal National Rose Society	http://www.roses.co.uk
Royal Society for the Prevention of Accidents	http://www.rospa.co.uk
Royal Society for the Protection of Birds	http://www.rspb.org
Sissinghurst	http://www.cincyflowershow.com/Pages/sissinghurst.html
Sissinghurst	http://www.enjoybritain.co.uk/counties/Kent/Sissinghurst135ise.cfm
Sissinghurst	http://www.woodhamhall.demon.co.uk/surround/siss.cast.html
Sissinghurst (Sisley Tour)	http://www.tka.co.uk/sisley/sisnghst.htm
Soil	http://www.hintze-online.com/sos/soils-online.html
Soil Chem	listproc@soils.umn.edu
Soils	listserv@unl.edu
Southern Water	http://www.southernwater.co.uk
Southport Flower Show	http://www.theflowershow.free.online.co.uk
Stanley Tools	http://www.stanleyworks.com/hand.htm
Stowe Landscape Garden	http://www.stowe.co.uk
Suite 101	http://suite101.com
Thomas Jefferson's Garden (US magazine)	http://www.bbg.org/gardening/kitchen/kitchen/hatch.html
Tile.Net Lists	http://tile.net/listserv
Tivoli Gardens, Copenhagen	http://www.tivoligardens.com/
Total Living Company	http://www.totalliving.com/totall.bin/menu/index.html?Jd8ul65osiF
Tree City Urban Forestry Mailing List	majordomo@dainet.de
Versailles 1	http://www.chateauversailles.fr
Versailles 2	http://members.dynasty.net/jmoats/versailles/index.htm
Virtual Garden	http://www.vg.com
Wagner Spray Tech	http://www.wagnerspraytech.co.uk/cordless.htm
Wallace Arnold Holidays	http://www.wallacearnold.com/home.htm
Waste	majordomo@cedar.univie.ac.at
Water Gardening In Texas	http://www.aggie-horticulture.tamu.edu/extension/homelandscape/watergarden
Wavedon Garden & Allotment Society	http://www.ncare.co.uk/wags/
Webferret search utility	http://www.ferretsoft.com/netferret/index.html
Whole Herb	http://www.storeybooks.com
Wiggly Wigglers	http://www.wigglywigglers.co.uk
Wisley (RHS)	http://www.rhs.org.uk/Around/gardens/gardens.asp
Worm Woman	http://www.wormwoman.com
Yahoo!	http://www.yahoo.co.uk
Yvoire (Le Jardin des Cinq Sens)	http://www.geneve-tourisme.ch/fr/decouvrir.html

. . . .

access provider – The company that provides you with access to the internet. This may be an independent provider or a large international organisation such as AOL or CompuServe. See also internet service provider.

ActiveX – A programming language that allows effects such as animations, games and other interactive features to be included a web page.

Adobe Acrobat – A type of software required for reading PDF files ('portable document format'). You may need to have Adobe Acrobat Reader when downloading large text files from the internet, such as lengthy reports or chapters from books. If your computer lacks it, the web page will prompt you, and usually offer you an immediate download of the free version.

address book – A directory in a web browser where you can store people's email addresses. This saves having to type them out each time you want to email someone. You just click on an address whenever you want it.

AltaVista – One of the half dozen most popular internet search engines. Just type in a few key words to find what you want on the internet: http://www.altasvista.com

AOL – America OnLine, the world's biggest internet service provider, with more than 20 million subscribers, and now merged with Time Warner. Because it has masses of content of its own – quite aside from the wider internet – it is sometimes referred to as an 'online' service provider rather than internet service provider. It has given away vast numbers of free CDs with the popular computer magazines to build its customer base.

applet – An application programmed in Java that is designed to run only on a web browser. Applets cannot read or write data onto your computer, only from the domain in which they are served from. When a web page using an applet is accessed, the browser will download it and run it on your computer. See also **Java.**

application – Any program, such as a word processor or spreadsheet program, designed for use on your computer.

ARPANET – Advanced Research Projects Agency Network, an early form of the internet.

ASCII – American Standard Code for Information Interchange. It is a simple text file format that can be accessed by most word processors and text editors. It is a universal file type for passing textual information across the internet.

Ask Jeeves – A popular internet search engine. Rather than just typing in a few key words for your search, you can type in a whole question or instruction, such as 'Find me everything about online investment.' It draws on a database of millions of questions and answers, and works best with fairly general questions.

ASP – Active Server Page, a filename extension for a type of web page.

attachment – A file sent with an email message. The attached file can be anything from a word-processed document to a database, spreadsheet, graphic, or even a sound or video file. For example you could email someone birthday greetings, and attach a sound track or video clip.

Authenticode – Authenticode is a system where ActiveX controls can be authenticated in some way, usually by a certificate.

avatar – A cartoon or image used to represent someone on screen while taking part in internet chat.

backup – A second copy of a file or a set of files. Backing up data is essential if there is any risk of data loss.

bandwidth – The width of the electronic highway that gives you access to the internet. The higher the bandwidth, the wider this highway, and the faster the traffic can flow.

banner ad – This is a band of text and graphics, usually situated at the top of a web page. It acts like a title, telling the user what the content of the page is about. It invites the visitor to click on it to visit that site. Banner advertising has become big business.

baud rate – The data transmission speed in a modem, measured in bps (bits per second).

BBS – Bulletin board service. A facility to read and to post public messages on a particular web site.

binary numbers – The numbering system used by computers. It only uses 1s and 0s to represent numbers.

Blue Ribbon Campaign – A widely supported campaign supporting free speech and opposing moves to censor the internet by all kinds of elected and unelected bodies.

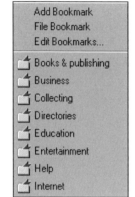

bookmark – A file of URLs of your favourite internet sites. Bookmarks are very easily created by bookmarking (mouse-clicking) any internet page you like the look of. If you are an avid user, you could soon end up with hundreds of them! In the Internet Explorer browser and AOL they are called 'favourites'.

boolean search – A search in which you type in words such as AND and OR to refine your search. Such words are called 'Boolean operators'. The concept is named after George Boole, a nineteenth-century English mathematician.

bot – Short for robot. It is used to refer to a program that will perform a task on the internet, such as carrying out a search.

browser – Your browser is your window to the internet, and is normally supplied by your internet service provider when you first sign up. It is the program that you use to access the world wide web, and manage your personal communications and privacy when online. By far the two most popular browsers are Netscape Communicator and its dominant rival Microsoft Internet Explorer. You can easily swap. Both can be downloaded free from their web sites and are found on the CD roms stuck to computer magazines. It won't make much difference which one you use – they both do much the same thing. Opera, at http://www.opera.com is a great alternative that improves security, is faster and more efficient.

bug – A weakness in a program or a computer system.

bulletin board – A type of computer-based news service that provides an email service and a file archive.

cache – A file storage area on a computer. Your web browser will normally cache (copy to your hard drive) each web page you visit. When you revisit that page on the web, you may in fact be looking at the page originally cached on your computer. To be sure you are viewing the current page, press **reload** – or **refresh** – on your browser toolbar. You can empty your cache from time to time, and the computer will do so automatically whenever the cache is full. In Internet Explorer, pages are saved in the Windows folder, Temporary Internet Files. In Netscape they are saved in a folder called 'cache'.

certificate – A computer file that securely identifies a person or organisation on the internet.

CGI (common gateway interface) – This defines how the web server should pass information to the program, such as what it's being asked to do, what objects it should work with, any inputs, and so on. It is the same for all web servers.

channel (chat) – Place where you can chat with other internet chatters. The name of a chat channel is prefixed with a hash mark, #.

click through – This is when someone clicks on a banner ad or other link, for example, and is moved from that page to the advertiser's web site.

client – This is the term given to the program that you use to access the internet.

For example your web browser is a web client, and your email program is an email client.

community – The internet is often described as a net community. This refers to the fact that many people like the feeling of belonging to a group of like-minded individuals. Many big web sites have been developed along these lines, such as GeoCities which is divided into special-interest 'neighbour-hoods', or America OnLine which is strong on member services.

compression – Computer files can be electronically compressed, so that they can be uploaded or downloaded more quickly across the internet, saving time and money. If an image file is compressed too much, there may be a loss of quality. To read them, you uncompress – 'unzip' – them.

content – Articles, columns, sales messages, images, and the text of your web site.

content services – Web sites dedicated to a particular subject.

cookie – A cookie is a small code that the server asks your browser to keep until it asks for it. If it sends it with the first page and asks for it back before each other page, they can follow you around the site, even if you switch your computer off in between.

cracker – Someone who breaks into computer systems with the intention of causing some kind of damage or abusing the system in some way.

crash – What happens when a computer program malfunctions. The operating system of your PC may perform incorrectly or come to a complete stop ('freeze'), forcing you to shut down and restart.

cross-posting – Posting an identical message in several different newgroups at the same time.

cybercash – This is a trademark, but is also often used as a broad term to describe the use of small payments made over the internet using a new form of electronic account that is loaded up with cash. You can send this money to the companies offering such cash facilities by cheque, or by credit card. Some internet companies offering travel-related items can accept electronic cash of this kind.

cyberspace – Popular term for the intangible 'place' where you go to surf – the ethereal and borderless world of computers and telecommunications on the internet.

cypherpunk – From the cypherpunk mailing list charter: 'Cypherpunks assume privacy is a good thing and wish there were more of it. Cypherpunks acknowledge that those who want privacy must create it for themselves and not expect governments, corporations, or other large, faceless organisations to grant them privacy out of beneficence. Cypherpunks know that people have been creating their own privacy for centuries with whispers, envelopes, closed doors, and couriers. Cypherpunks do not seek to prevent other people from speaking about their experiences or their opinions.'

cypherpunk remailer – Cypherpunk remailers strip headers from the messages and add new ones.

data – Information. Data can exist in many forms such as numbers in a spreadsheet, text in a document, or as binary numbers stored in a computer's memory.

dial up account – This allows you to connect your computer to your internet provider's computer remotely.

digital – Based on the two binary digits, 1 and 0. The operation of all computers is based on this amazingly simple concept. All forms of information are capable of being digitalised – numbers, words, and even sounds and images – and then transmitted over the internet.

directory – On a PC, a folder containing your files.

DNS – Domain name server.

Dial-Up Networking

Glossary

domain name – A name that identifies an IP address. It identifies to the computers on the rest of the internet where to access particular information. Each domain has a name. For someone@somewhere.co.uk, 'somewhere' is the domain name. The domain name for Internet Handbooks for instance is: www.internet-handbooks.co.uk

download – 'Downloading' means copying a file from one computer on the internet to your own computer. You do this by clicking on a button that links you to the appropriate file. Downloading is an automatic process, except you have to click 'yes' to accept the download and give it a file name. You can download any type of file – text, graphics, sound, spreadsheet, computer programs, and so on.

ebusiness – The broad concept of doing business to business, and business to consumer sales, over the internet.

ecommerce – The various means and techniques of transacting business on-line.

email – Electronic mail, any message or file you send from your computer to another computer using your 'email client' program (such as Netscape Messenger or Microsoft Outlook).

email address – The unique address given to you by your ISP. It can be used by others using the internet to send email messages to you. An example of a standard email address is: mybusiness@aol.com

email bomb – An attack by email where you are sent hundreds or thousands of email messages in a very short period. This attack often prevents you receiving genuine email messages.

emoticons – Popular symbols used to express emotions in email. Emoticons are not normally appropriate for business communications. The best known is smiley :-) which means 'I'm smiling!'

encryption – The scrambling of information to make it unreadable without a key or password. Email and any other data can now be encrypted using PGP and other freely available programs. Modern encryption has become so powerful as to be to all intents and purposes uncrackable. Law enforcers worldwide want access to people's and organisation's passwords and security keys.

Excite – A popular internet directory and search engine used to find pages relating to specific keywords which you enter. See also Yahoo!.

ezines   The term for magazines and newsletters published on the internet.

FAQ – Frequently asked questions. You will see 'FAQ' everywhere you go on the internet. If you are ever doubtful about anything check the FAQ page, if the site has one, and you should find the answers to your queries.

favorites – The rather coy term for **bookmarks** – used by Internet Explorer, and by America Online. Maintaining a list of 'favourites' is designed to make returning to a site easier.

file – A file is any body of data such as a word processed document, a spreadsheet, a database file, a graphics or video file, sound file, or computer program.

filtering software – Software loaded onto a computer to prevent access by someone to unwelcome content on the internet, notably porn. The well-known 'parental controls' include CyberSitter, CyberPatrol, SurfWatch and NetNanny. They can be blunt instruments. For example, if they are programmed to reject all web pages containing the word 'virgin', you would not be able to access any web page hosted at Richard Branson's Virgin Net! Of course, there are also web sites that tell you step-by-step how to disable or bypass these filtering tools.

finger – A chat command which returns information about the other chat user, including idle time (time since they last did anything). Also, a tool for locating people on the internet. The most common use is to see if a person has an account at a particular internet site.

firewall – A firewall is special security software designed to stop the flow of certain files into and out of a computer network, e.g. viruses or attacks by hackers. A firewall would be an important feature of any fully commercial web site.

flame – A hostile or aggressive message posted in a newsgroup or to an individual newsgroup user. If they get out of hand there can be flame wars.

folder – The name for a directory on a computer. It is a place in which files are stored.

form – A web page that allows or requires you to enter information into fields on the page and send the information to a web site, program or individual on the web. Forms are often used for registration or sending questions and comments to web sites.

forums – Places for discussion on the internet. They include Usenet newsgroups, mailing lists, and bulletin board services.

frames – A web design feature in which web pages are divided into several areas or panels, each containing separate information. A typical set of frames in a page includes an index frame (with navigation links), a banner frame (for a heading), and a body frame (for text matter).

freebies – The 'give away' products, services or other enticements offered on a web site to attract registrations.

freespace – An allocation of free web space by an internet service provider or other organisation, to its users or subscribers.

freeware – Software programs made available without charge. Where a small charge is requested, the term is **shareware.**

front page – The first page of your web site that the visitor will see. FrontPage is also the name of a popular web authoring package from Microsoft.

FTP – File transfer protocol – the method the internet uses to speed files back and forth between computers. Your browser will automatically select this method, for instance, when you want to download your bank statements to reconcile your accounts. In practice you don't need to worry about FTP unless you are thinking about creating and publishing your own web pages: then you would need some of the freely available FTP software. Despite the name, it's easy to use.

GIF – 'Graphic interchange format', a very common type of graphic file. It is a compressed file format used on web pages and elsewhere to display files that contain graphic images. See also JPEG.

graphical client – A graphical client typically uses many windows, one for each conversation you are involved in. Each window has a command line and status bar.

GUI – Short for graphic user interface. It describes the user-friendly screens found in Windows and other WIMP environments (Windows, icons, mice, pointers).

hacker – A person interested in computer programming, operating systems, the internet and computer security. The term can be used to describe a person who breaks into computer systems with the intention of pointing out the weaknesses in a system. In common usage, the term is often wrongly used to describe crackers.

header – The header is that part of a message which contains information about the sender and the route that the message took through the internet.

history list – A record of visited web pages. Your browser probably includes a history list. It is handy way of revisiting sites whose addresses you have forgotten to bookmark – just click on the item you want in the history list. You can normally delete all or part of the history list in your browser. However, your ISP may well be keeping a copy of this information (see **internet**

service providers above).

hit counter – A piece of software used by a web site to publicly display the number of hits it has received.

hits – The number of times a web page has been viewed.

home page – This refers to the index page of an individual or an organisation on the internet. It usually contains links to related pages of information, and to other relevant sites.

host – A host is any computer where a particular file or domain is stored, and from where people can retrieve or access it.

HotBot – A popular internet search engine used to find pages relating to any keywords you decide to enter.

HTML – Hyper text markup language, the universal computer language used to create pages on the world wide web. It is much like word processing, but uses special 'tags' for formatting the text and creating hyperlinks to other web pages.

HTTP – Hypertext transfer protocol, the technical rules on which the world wide web is based. It is the language spoken between your browser and the web servers. It is the standard way that HTML documents are transferred from a host computer to your local browser when you're surfing the internet. You'll see the http acronym at the start of every web address, for example:

http://www.abcxyz.com

With modern browsers, it is no longer necessary to enter 'http://' at the start of the address. See also FTP.

hyperlink – See **link.**

hypertext – This is a link on an HTML page that, when clicked with a mouse, results in a further HTML page or graphic being loaded into view on your browser.

Infoseek – One of the ten most popular internet search engines.

internet – The broad term for the fast-expanding network of global computers that can access each other in seconds by phone and satellite links. If you are using a modem on your computer, you too are part of the internet. The general term 'internet' encompasses email, web pages, internet chat, newsgroups, and video conferencing. It is rather like the way we speak of 'the printed word' when we mean books, magazines, newspapers, newsletters, catalogues, leaflets, tickets and posters. The 'internet' does not exist in one place any more than 'the printed word' does.

Internet 2 – A new version of the internet being developed in the USA, intended for exclusive use by academic institutions and their members.

internet account – The account set up by your internet service provider which gives you access to the world wide web, electronic mail facilities, newsgroups and other value added services.

Internet Explorer – The world's most popular browser software, a product of MicroSoft and leading the field against Netscape (now owned by America OnLine).

internet service providers – ISPs are commercial, educational or official organisations which offer people ('users') access to the internet. The well-known ones in the UK include AOL, CompuServe, BT Internet, Freeserve, Demon and Virgin Net. Commercial ISPs may levy a fixed monthly charge, though the world wide trend is now towards free services. Services typically include access to the world wide web, email and newsgroups, as well as news, chat, and entertainment. Your internet service provider may know everything you do on the internet – emails you send and receive, the web sites you visit, information you downloaded, key words you type into search engines, newsgroups you visit and messages you read and post.

Internic – One of the bodies responsible for allocating and maintaining internet domain names: http://www.internic.net

intranet – A private computer network that uses internet technology to allow communication between individuals, for example within a large commercial organisation. It often operates on a LAN (local area network).

IP address – An 'internet protocol' address. All computers linked to the internet have one. The address is somewhat like a telephone number, and consists of four sets of numbers separated by dots.

IRC – Internet relay chat. Chat is an enormously popular part of the internet, and there are all kinds of chat rooms and chat software. The chat involves typing messages which are sent and read in real time. It was developed in 1988 by a Finn called Jarkko Oikarinen.

ISDN – Integrated Services Digital Network. This is a high-speed telephone network that can send computer data from the internet to your PC faster than a normal telephone line.

Java – A programming language developed by Sun Microsystems to use the special properties of the internet to create graphics and multimedia applications on web sites.

JavaScript – A simple programming language that can be put onto a web page to create interactive effects such as buttons that change appearance when you position the mouse over them.

jpeg – The acronym is short for Joint Photographic Experts Group. A JPEG is a specialised file format used to display graphic files on the internet. JPEG files are smaller than similar GIF files and so have become ever more popular – even though there is sometimes a feeling that their quality is not as good as GIF format files. See also MPEG.

key shortcut – Two keys pressed at the same time. Usually the 'control' key (Ctrl), 'Alt' key, or 'Shift' key combined with a letter or number. For example to use 'Control-D', press 'Control', tap the 'D' key once firmly then take your finger off the 'Control' key.

keywords – Words that sum up your web site for being indexed in search engines. For example for a cosmetic site the key words might include beauty, lipstick, make-up, fashion, cosmetic and so on.

kick – To eject someone from a chat channel.

LAN – A local area network, a computer network usually located in one building or campus.

link – A hypertext phrase or image that calls up another web page when you click on it. Most web sites have lots of hyperlinks, or 'links' for short. These appear on the screen as buttons, images or bits of text (often underlined) that you can click on with your mouse to jump to another site on the world wide web.

Linux – A freely available operating system for personal computers, and a potentially serious challenger to Microsoft Windows. Developed on DIY lines as open source software, it has developed a growing following.

listserver – An automated email system whereby subscribers are able to receive and send email from other subscribers to the list.

log on – You may be asked to 'log on' to certain sites and particular pages. This normally means entering your user ID in the form of a name and a password.

log on/log off – To access/leave a network. In the early days of computing this literally involved writing a record in a log book.

lurk – The slang term used to describe reading a newsgroup's messages without actually taking part in that newsgroup. Despite the connotations of the word, it is a perfectly respectable activity on the internet.

macros – 'Macro languages' are used to automate repetitive tasks in Word processors.

mail server – A remote computer through which you can send and receive emails. Your internet access provider will usually act as your mail server.

mailing list – A forum where messages are distributed by email to the members of the forum. The two types of lists are discussion and announcement. Discussion lists allow exchange between list members. Announcement lists are one-way only and used to distribute information such as news or humour. A good place to find mailing lists is Liszt (http://www.liszt.com). You can normally quit a mailing list by sending an email message to request removal.

marquee – A moving (scrolling) line of text, banner or other graphic on a web site, normally used for advertising purposes.

Media player – Software on a personal computer that will play sounds and images including video clips and animations.

metasearch engine – A site that sends a keyword search to many different search engines and directories so you can use many search engines from one place.

meta tags – The technical term for the keywords used in your web page code to help search engine software rank your site.

Mixmaster – An anonymous remailer that sends and receives email messages as packages of exactly the same size and often randomly varies the delay time between receiving and remailing to make interception harder.

modem – This is an internal or external piece of hardware plugged into your PC. It links into a standard phone socket, thereby connecting your computer to the internet. The word derives from MOdulator/DEModulator.

moderator – A person in charge of a mailing list, newsgroup or forum. The moderator prevents unwanted messages.

mpeg – or **mpg** – The file format used for video clips available on the internet. See also JPEG.

MP3 – An immensely popular audio format that allows you to download and play music on your computer. It compresses music to create files that are small yet whose quality is almost as good as CD music. See http://mpeg.org for further technical information, or the consumer web site www.mp3.com. At time of writing, MP4, even faster to download was being developed.

MUDs – Multi-User Dungeons, interactive chat-based fantasy world games. Popular in the early days of the internet, they are in now in decline with the advance of networked arcade games such as Quake and Doom.

navigate – To click on the hyperlinks on a web site in order to move to other web pages or internet sites.

net – A slang term for the internet. In the same way, the world wide web is often just called the web.

netiquette – Popular term for the unofficial rules and language people follow to keep electronic communication in an acceptably polite form.

Netmeeting – This Microsoft plug in allows a moving video picture to be contained within a web page. It is now integrated into Windows Media Player.

Netscape – After Microsoft's Internet Explorer, Netscape is the most popular browser software available for surfing the internet. An excellent browser, Netscape has suffered in the wake of Internet Explorer, mainly because of the success of Microsoft in getting the latter pre-loaded on most new PCs. Netscape Communicator comes complete with email, newsgroups, address book and bookmarks, plus a web page composer, and you can adjust its settings in all sorts of useful ways. Netscape was taken over by American Online for $4 billion.

nettie – Slang term for someone who likes to spend a lot of time on the internet.

newbie – Popular term for a new member of a newsgroup or mailing list.

newsgroup – A Usenet discussion group. Each newsgroup is a collection of messages, usually unedited and not checked by anyone ('unmoderated'). Messages can be placed within the newsgroup by anyone including you. It is rather like reading and sending public emails. The ever-growing newsgroups have been around for much longer than the world wide web, and are an endless source of information, gossip, news, entertainment, sex, politics, resources and ideas. The 80,000-plus newsgroups are collectively referred to as Usenet, and millions of people use it every day.

news reader – A type of software that enables you to search, read, post and manage messages in a newsgroup. It will normally be supplied by your internet service provider when you first sign up, or preloaded on your new computer. The best known are Microsoft Outlook Express, and Netscape Messenger.

news server – A remote computer (e.g. your internet service provider) that enables you to access the newsgroups on Usenet. If you cannot get some or any newsgroups from your existing news server, use your favourite search engine to search for 'open news servers' – there are lots of them freely available. When you have found one you like, add it to your news reader by clicking on its name. The first time you do this, it may take 10 to 20 minutes to load the names of all the newsgroups onto your computer, but after that they open up in seconds whenever you want them.

nick – Nickname, an alias you can give yourself and use when entering a chat channel, rather than using your real name.

Nominet – An official body for registering domain names in the UK (for example web sites whose name ends in .co.uk).

online – The time you spend linked via a modem to the internet. You can keep your phone bill down by reducing online time. The opposite term is offline.

open source software – A type of freely modifiable software, such as Linux. A definition and more information can be found at: www.opensource.org

OS – The operating system in a computer, for example MS DOS (Microsoft Disk Operating System), or Windows 95/98/2000.

packet – The term for any small piece of data sent or received over the internet on your behalf by your internet service provider, and containing your address and the recipient's address. One email message for example may be transmitted as several different packets of information, and reassembled at the other end to recreate the message.

password – A word or series of letters and numbers that enables a user to access a file, computer or program. A passphrase is a password made by using more than one word.

PC – Personal computer.

PDA – Personal Data Assistant – a mobile phone, palm top or any other hand-held processor, typically used to access the internet

Pentium – The name of a very popular microprocessor chip in personal computers, manufactured by Intel. The first Pentium IIIs were supplied with secret and unique personal identifiers, which ordinary people surfing the net were unwittingly sending out, enabling persons unknown to construct detailed user profiles. After a storm of protest, Pentium changed the technology so that this identifier could be disabled. If you buy or use a Pentium III computer you should be aware of this risk to your privacy when online.

PGP – Pretty Good Privacy. A proprietary method of encoding a message before transmitting it over the internet. With PGP, a message is first compressed then encoded with the help of keys. Just like the valuables in a locked safe, your message is safe unless a person has access to the right keys. Some governments are now demanding permanent access to people's private keys.

ping – You can use a ping test to check the connection speed between your computer and another computer.

Glossary ....

plug in – A type of (usually free and downloadable) software required to add some form of functionality to web page viewing. A well-known example is Macromedia Shockwave, a plug in which enables you to view animations.

PoP – Point of presence. This refers to the dial up phone numbers available from your ISP. If your ISP does not have a local point of presence (i.e. local access phone number), then don't sign up – your telephone bill will rocket because you will be charged national phone rates. All the major ISPs have local numbers covering the whole of the country.

portal site – Portal means gateway. It is a web site designed to be used as a starting point for your web experience each time you go online. Portals often serve as general information points and offer news, weather and other information that you can customise to your own needs. Yahoo! is a good example of a portal (http://www.yahoo.com). A portal site includes the one that loads into your browser each time you connect to the internet. It could for example be the front page of your internet service provider. Or you can set your browser to make it some other front page, for example a search engine such as AltaVista, or even your own home page if you have one.

post, to – The common term used for sending ('posting') messages to a newsgroup. Posting messages is very like sending emails, except of course that they are public and everyone can read them. Also, newsgroup postings are archived, and can be read by anyone in the world years later. Because of this, many people feel more comfortable using an 'alias' (made-up name) when posting messages.

privacy – You have practically no personal privacy online. Almost every mouse click and key stroke you make while online is being electronically logged, analysed and possibly archived by internet organisations, government agencies, police and other surveillance services. You are also leaving a permanent trail of data on whichever computer you are using. But then, if you have nothing to hide you have nothing to fear from 'big brother'. To explore privacy issues worldwide visit the authoritative Electronic Frontier Foundation web site at www.eff.org, and for the UK, www.netfreedom.org

protocol – Technical term for the method by which computers communicate. A protocol is an agreed set of technical rules that can be used between systems. For example, for viewing web pages your computer would use hypertext transfer protocol (http). For downloading and uploading files, it would use file transfer protocol (ftp). It's not something to worry about in ordinary life.

proxy – An intermediate computer or server, used for reasons of security.

Quicktime – A popular free software program from Apple Computers. It is designed to play sounds and images including video clips and animations on both Apple Macs and personal computers.

radio button – A button which, when clicked, looks like this: ◉

refresh, reload – The refresh or reload button on your browser toolbar tells the web page you are looking at to reload.

register – You may have to give your name, personal details and financial information to some sites before you can continue to use the pages. Site owners may want to produce a mailing list to offer you products and services. Registration is also used to discourage casual traffic which can clog up access.

registered user – Someone who has filled out an online form and then been granted permission to access a restricted area of a web site. Access is usually obtained by logging on, typically by entering a password and user name.

remailer – A remailer preserves your privacy by acting as a go-between when you browse or send email messages. An anonymous remailer is simply a computer connected to the internet that can forward an email message to other people after stripping off the header of the messages. Once a message is routed through an anonymous remailer, the recipient of that message, or anyone intercepting it, can no longer identify its origin.

RSA – A popular method of encryption, and used in Netscape browsers. See http://www.rsa.com and see also PGP above.

router – A machine that directs – 'routes' – internet data (network packets) from one place to another.

rules – The term for message filters in Outlook Express.

search engine – A search engine is a web site you can use for finding something on the internet. Popular search engines are big web sites and information directories in their own right. There are hundreds of them; the best known include Alta Vista, Excite, Google, Infoseek, Lycos and Yahoo!.

secure servers – The hardware and software provided so that people can use their credit cards and leave other details without the risk of others seeing them online. Your browser will tell you when you are entering a secure site.

secure sockets layer (SSL) – A standard piece of technology which encrypts and secures financial transactions and data flow over the internet.

security certificate – Information used by the SSL protocol to establish a secure connection. Security certificates contain information about who it belongs to, who it was issued by, some form of unique identification, valid dates, and an encrypted fingerprint that can be used to verify the contents of the certificate. In order for an SSL connection to be created both sides must have a valid security certificate.

server – Any computer on a network that provides access and serves information to other computers.

shareware – Software that you can try before you buy. Usually there is some kind of limitation such as an expiry date. To get the registered version, you must pay for the software, typically $20 to $40. A vast amount of shareware is now available on the internet.

Shockwave – A popular piece of software produced by Macromedia, which enables you to view animations and other special effects on web sites. You can download it free and in a few minutes from Macromedia's web site. The effects can be fun, but they slow down the speed at which the pages load into your browser window.

signature file – This is a little text file in which you can place your address details, for adding to email and newsgroup messages. Once you have created a signature file, it is appended automatically to your emails. You can of delete or edit it whenever you like.

Slashdot – One of the leading technology news web sites, found at: http://slashdot.org

smiley – A form of **emoticon**.

snail mail – The popular term for the standard postal service involving postpersons, vans, trains, planes, sacks and sorting offices.

spam – The popular term for electronic junk mail – unsolicited and unwelcome email messages sent across the internet. There are various forms of spambusting software which you can now obtain to filter out unwanted email messages.

sniffer – A program on a computer system (usually an ISP's system) designed to collect information about how people use the internet. Sniffers are often used by hackers to collect passwords and user names.

SSL – Secure socket layer, a key part of internet security technology.

subscribe – The term for accessing a newsgroup in order to read and post messages in the newsgroup. There is no charge, and you can subscribe, unsubscribe and resubscribe at will with a click of your mouse. Unless you post a message, no-one in the newsgroup will know that you have subscribed or unsubscribed.

Glossary ....

surfing – Slang term for browsing the internet, especially following trails of links on pages across the world wide web.

sysop – Systems operator, someone rather like a moderator for example of a chat room or bulletin board service.

TCP/IP – Transmission control protocol/internet protocol, the essential technology of the internet. It's not normally something to worry about.

telnet – Software that allows you to connect via the internet to a remote computer and work as if you were a terminal linked to that system.

theme – A term in web page design. A theme describes the general colours and graphics used within a web site. Many themes are available in the form of readymade templates.

thumbnail – A small version of a graphic file which, when clicked, expands to full size.

thread – An ongoing topic in a Usenet newsgroup or mailing list discussion. The term refers to the original message on a particular topic, and all the replies and other messages which spin off from it. With news reading software, you can easily 'view thread' and thus read the related messages in one convenient batch.

traceroute – A program that traces the route of a communication between your machine and a remote system. It is useful if you need to discover a person's ISP, for example in the case of a spammer.

traffic – The amount of data flowing across the internet to a particular web site, newsgroup or chat room, or as emails.

trojan horse – A program that seems to perform a useful task but is really a malevolent one designed to cause damage to a computer system.

uploading – The act of copying files from your PC to a server or other PC on the internet, for example when you are publishing your own web pages. The term is most commonly used to describe the act of copying HTML pages onto the internet via FTP.

UNIX – This is a computer operating system that has been in use for many years, and still is used in many larger systems. Most ISPs use it.

URL – Uniform resource locator – the address of each internet page. For instance the URL of Internet Handbooks is http://www.internet-handbooks.co.uk

Usenet – The collection of well over 50,000 active newsgroups that make up a substantial part of the internet.

virtual reality – The presentation of a lifelike scenario in electronic form. It can be used for gaming, business or educational purposes.

virus – A computer program maliciously designed to cause havoc to people's computer files. Viruses can typically be received when downloading program files from the internet, or from copying material from infected disks. Even Word files can now be infected. You can protect yourself from the vast majority of them by installing some inexpensive anti-virus software, such as Norton, McAfee or Dr Solomon.

WAP – Wireless Application Protocol, the new technology that enables mobile phones to access the internet. Traditional web sites are facing the challenge of 'wapalisation'.

web authoring – Creating HTML pages to upload onto the internet. You will be a web author if you create your own home page for uploading onto the internet.

web client – Another term for a browser such as Internet Explorer or Netscape Navigator.

Webcrawler – A popular internet search engine used to find pages relating to specific keywords entered.

webmaster – Any person who manages a web site.

web page – Any single page of information you can view on the world wide web. A typical web page includes a unique URL (address), headings, text, images, and hyperlinks (usually in the form of graphic icons, or underlined text). One web page usually contains links to lots of other web pages, either within the same web site or elsewhere on the world wide web.

web rings – A network of interlinked web sites that share a common interest.

whois – A network service that allows you to consult a database containing information about someone. A whois query can, for example, help to find the identity of someone who is sending you unwanted email messages.

Windows – The ubiquitous operating system for personal computers developed by Bill Gates and the Microsoft Corporation. The Windows 3.1 version was followed by Windows 95, further enhanced by Windows 98. Windows 2000 is the latest.

WWW – The world wide web. Since it began in 1994 this has become the most popular part of the internet. The web is now made up of more than a billion web pages of every imaginable description, typically linking to other pages. Developed by the British computer scientist, Tim Berners-Lee, its growth has been exponential and is set to continue so.

WYSIWYG – 'What you see is what you get.' If you see it on the screen, then it should look just the same when you print it out.

Yahoo! – Probably the world's most popular internet directory and search engine, and now valued on Wall Street at billions of dollars: http://www.yahoo.com

zip/unzip – Many files that you download from the internet will be in compressed format, especially if they are large files. This is to make them quicker to download. These files are said to be zipped or compressed. Unzipping these compressed files means returning them to their original size on receipt. Zip files have the extension '.zip' and are created (and unzipped) using WinZip or a similar popular software package.

Visit the free Internet HelpZone at
www.internet-handbooks.co.uk
Helping you master the internet

Index

Index...